Hotel Secrets
from the
Travel Detective

Also by Peter Greenberg

The Travel Detective Flight Crew Confidential:
People Who Fly for a Living Reveal Insider
Secrets and Hidden Values in Cities
and Airports Around the World

The Travel Detective:
How to Get the Best Service
and the Best Deals from Airlines, Hotels,
Cruise Ships, and Car Rental Agencies

Hotel Secrets
from the
Travel Detective

Insider Tips on Getting
the Best Value, Service, and Security
in Accommodations
from Bed-and-Breakfasts
to Five-Star Resorts

Peter Greenberg

VILLARD  NEW YORK

To the thousands of hoteliers, maids, doormen, bellhops, engineers, designers, bartenders, concierges, and chefs who allow me to still feel at home wherever I am in the world

Acknowledgments

All saints can do miracles, but few of them can keep a hotel.
— *St. Francis of Assisi*

This page is, as I'm sure you'll understand, intentionally incomplete. To research and report this book, I've spoken to dozens of hotel owners and general managers, maids and security officers, doormen and engineers, asset managers and concierges, bellmen (and women) and chefs, check-in clerks and police officers, lawyers, and yes, guests.

Because of the nature of this book and the agreements I made when I did these interviews, I cannot officially acknowledge most of these people by name. In many cases, they took a risk by talking. They shared with me sensitive information and revealed important details about the process and business of hotels. They agreed to trust me, and they have my thanks. Without them, this book could not have been done.

But I *can* effusively thank my research team by name: my assistant, Jill Gable, and researchers Cheryl Chaney, Robin Bowens, Ranesha Mattu, also Erin Papworth. A special thanks to Isabel Gonzalez for all her help in researching so many of the hotel rooms with a past. Aaron Kenedi helped with the final research and organization. This book could never have been completed without the discerning eye of Ginny Carroll, who asked the right questions in all the right places. My agent Amy Rennert was persistent in keeping me focused, and deserves special praise for her editorial work. Thanks, too, to her assistant Chris Gruener. And then there's my editor, Bruce Tracy, whose editorial guidance as well as patience in waiting for this book to be finished made a huge difference.

Thanks also go to Betsy Alexander of the *Today* show, who really knows a good idea when she hears it, and to everyone in the NBC news family who understands that travel is indeed news and then allows me to treat it that way.

Contents

CHAPTER 13
Additional Resources   251

Hotel Secrets
from the
Travel Detective

CHAPTER 1

My Life in Hotels

People travel for the same reason as they collect
works of art: because the best people do it.

—*Aldous Huxley*

have been traveling and staying in hotels since I was six months old. I've stayed—and, some might argue, I have lived—in hotels most of my adult life. At the very least, hotels could be considered my second home, and certain ones qualify me for near permanent residence status.

My official residence is Los Angeles, but in the past three years, I have spent an average of forty-seven nights a year there, few of them even consecutive. I have made the acquaintance of some of my neighbors in Los Angeles, but I know all of the bell and front desk staff at the Mark Hotel and Essex House hotels in New York, the Athenaeum in London, the Regent and the Oriental in Bangkok. When I check into these hotels, the staff often greets me by saying, "Welcome home." I *feel* at home in hotels.

Indeed, hotels are where we live much of our personal history. In nineteenth- and twentieth-century literature, so many of the modern mythical heroes eventually turn up at one of the great hotels. Murders, love affairs, business intrigue, and political negotiations, ranging from acts of war to declarations of surrender, happen at hotels. The players include arms merchants and divas, journalists and boxers, traveling salesmen like Willy Loman, and real-life characters like Ernest Hemingway. Each has his or her own special relationship with hotels.

Hotels evolved as transportation options grew, and the types of hotels became as distinct as the fast-changing and different types of people who started to visit them. Butchers, bakers, and candlestick makers—as well as the owners of their businesses—came to stay.

Small inns were eclipsed by skyscrapers like the Waldorf-Astoria in New York, railroad hotels in Canada dwarfed the terminals they served, and a new form of grand hotel architecture was accelerated by the appearance of hotels like the Savoy in

London and the Ritz in Paris. It's been argued that the grand hotel was one of the great innovations of the Industrial Revolution—a visible reflection and a symbol of an elevated society, as much seduced by service as demanding of it.

With every grand hotel came not only pomp and circumstance but a sense of entitlement. If you were in the lobby, you presumably had reason to be there. If you actually had a room at the hotel, you belonged. Joan Didion once wrote that "great hotels have always been social ideas, flawless mirrors to the particular societies they service." And that same sense of entitlement and service endures today.

> **OLDEST HOTEL:** The Hoshi Ryokan in the village of Awazu, Japan, is the world's oldest hotel. It dates back to A.D. 717, when an inn was built near a hot-water spring said to have miraculous healing properties. The waters are still celebrated for their recuperative effects, and the Ryokan now has one hundred bedrooms.

Hotels still loom larger than life to me. One of the first books I read was Kay Thompson's *Eloise*, which allowed me to fantasize about the wonderful exploits of this marvelous child who lived at the Plaza Hotel in New York. I remember my first visit to the Plaza, when all I could do was look up because it was the biggest thing I'd ever seen. I felt privileged to be there—and one reason was that my mother *told* me I was privileged to be there.

A hotel is much more than simply bricks and mortar housing bedrooms. It is a living, breathing entity, a welcoming edifice where the front door is never locked. "You must suspend reality when you are in a hotel," says Jon Tisch, CEO of the Loews hotels, "because you are placing your trust and safety in the hands of others."

The hotel concept is a fairly recent one. In colonial Boston, travelers found rest not in hotels or motels, but at local taverns and inns. Since women rarely took to the road in those days, colonial men generally frequented these roadside taverns. They slept in rustic bedrooms—often sharing beds—after spending considerable time drinking pints of beer. These taverns were centers for male bonding and conversation, and, in periods of unrest or revolution, they were the hubs for secret political meetings.

As these precursors to the modern hotel developed beyond simple taprooms, they began to be known as "houses"—a gen-

---

MOST EXPENSIVE HOTEL ROOM: The world's most expensive hotel room is the Imperial Suite at the President Wilson Hotel in Geneva, Switzerland, which can be reserved for the princely sum of $33,000 per night. The suite, which is accessed by a private elevator, takes up an entire floor of the Starwood Luxury Collection hotel. It has bulletproof windows and doors and four bedrooms, all of which overlook Lake Geneva. The master bedroom boasts a dressing room and a study. The oval mahogany table in the dining room seats twenty-six guests, and the living room contains a billiards table, a cocktail lounge, and a library.

SECOND PLACE GOES TO: The Royal Suite at the Grand Resort Lagonissi in Athens, Greece. For $25,600 a night, guests get an indoor pool, a steam room, a sauna, a dining room, a private massage room, a private business center, and a private dock.

THIRD PLACE GOES TO: The Bridge Suite at the Atlantis in the Bahamas. For a mere $25,000 a night, guests get a bar lounge, an entertainment center, a kitchen, and the services of a butler.

tler title for a much-improved environment. During the second quarter of the nineteenth century, an increasing number of travelers arrived in Boston by coach or ship, and lodging and dining houses proliferated throughout the city, many bearing patriotic names such as the American House, the Shawmut, the Adams, the Revere House. Boston's resident houses became so genteel—and, sometimes, so luxurious—that even ladies were ably accommodated.

Today, of course, the numbers of and the demographics for hotels are as staggering as they are different. In the past decade, there has been unprecedented growth in the hotel business. In 1990 there were a reported 2.5 million hotel/motel guest rooms in the United States. The most recent room census indicates that the total now exceeds 4.4 million rooms.

HIGHEST-ALTITUDE HOTEL: The Everest View Hotel above Namche, Nepal—the village closest to Everest base camp—is at a record thirteen thousand feet above sea level.

Baby boomers (age 35 to 54) generate more travel than any other age group in the United States, registering more than 241 million trips last year. Many baby boomer travelers spend a substantial amount on their trips—14 percent pay $1,000 or more for a vacation, excluding the cost of transportation. People in this group are also more likely to stay in hotels or motels, travel for business, and fly to their destinations.

The Federal Aviation Administration (FAA) reports that at any given hour, there are sixty-one thousand people airborne over the United States, and a majority of them are headed for a hotel when they land. Thousands more travel by car to their destinations, which, more often than not, include hotels. In fact, on an average day the travel industry sells 2.5 million hotel rooms.

NORTHERNMOST HOTEL: The world's most northerly hotel is the Svalbard Polar Hotel (now known as the Radisson SAS Polar Hotel) in Longyearbyen, Svalbard, Norway, at a latitude of 78°13'N.

If recent history and experience are any indication, by the time we get to the front desk of any hotel, we've already been abused by the airline travel experience to such an extent that we arrive feeling either like refugees not wanting to be beaten anymore or like Rambo on a mission—and taking no prisoners.

At that point, many hotel executives fail to see that they are in an enviable position: they have the power to completely turn things around and make it not only better for their guests, but truly memorable.

Of course, most don't seize that opportunity, and that's what this book is all about: how to have a memorable hotel experience. It reveals the inside process of hotels, their design, and the obstacles to having a good stay. In short, this book teaches you the finesse you need to improve your hotel experience—to not only perceive but also *receive* value. Believe it or not, this is not only possible—it is *doable*, virtually every time you travel and stay in a hotel.

I wrote the first Travel Detective book (*The Travel Detective: How to Get the Best Services and the Best Deals from Airlines, Hotels, Cruise Ships, and Car Rental Agencies,* Random House, 2001) as a sort of manifesto and inside guide to beating the airlines (and, yes, some hotels) at their own game, playing by *their* rules. But in recent years, there's been an unfortunate trend, as many hotels apparently follow the airline model of customer service, turning the hotel experience into a commodity.

I contend that there has been a paradigm change in the way we travel and in the expectations we have when we travel. First, travel is no longer about just the destination, it's also about the experience. In fact, for many of us, the destination has become incidental to the experience. That experience is the focus of this book.

Perhaps it's more useful to describe what this book is *not* about. It's not about just the price of hotel rooms and how to get a great deal. Rather, it helps you avoid the frustrations involved in the process of first finding and then staying in a hotel—and it helps you maximize the value of your stay once you are there, especially in terms of service.

CHAPTER 2

Who Do You Trust?

t's a matter of distribution channels. Which—or how many—do you choose in selecting a hotel? And which do hoteliers choose to distribute their inventory? Let's start with toll-free reservation lines.

I have always argued that you should never call a toll-free reservation number to book a room. With few exceptions, these phone numbers connect you to a central reservations clearinghouse, and the person on the other end of the line has no power or discretion to alter the quoted rate. In many cases, the rooms available from hotels that use these clearinghouses are priced much higher than the same rooms offered to people who simply walk into a hotel or call the hotel directly.

But calling the hotel directly can also be problematic. If you invest a dollar or two in long-distance charges and call the hotel directly, you're in trouble if you simply ask for reservations—in most cases, your call is rerouted to that clearinghouse. Instead, you need to speak directly to the hotel's general manager, the MOD (manager on duty), or the director of sales.

However, there is an alternative to making your own hotel reservations: you can use the services of a travel agent.

THE TRAVEL AGENT RELATIONSHIP

Many people still depend on travel agents to book their rooms, especially at pricier hotels and resorts where guests expect to get not just a room but that memorable experience I've described.

Most people who still use travel agents claim to do so because of the convenience. But there are other factors at work in that travel agent–traveler relationship.

Travel agents remain a key source of business for premium

and luxury hotels, but the role of a good agent has changed considerably in the past ten years. "Before the Internet," says Matthew Upchurch, who runs Virtuoso, the powerful consortium of top-tier travel agents, "agents were needed to give their clients hotel options and recommendations, presented with brochures from the recommended hotels. These days," he explains, "the Internet is great for providing tons of hotel options and ways to reserve them. But while the Internet has made information more instantaneous, in many ways it hasn't made the selection of a hotel any easier."

He's right. Why? Most travel websites are merely online brochures, and everyone knows that the information in brochures should be taken with a big grain of salt. "A brochure won't tell you if the room furnishings are tired," Upchurch says, "if the property is undergoing noisy construction, or if there's a convention of *Star Trek* devotees booked there for the same time period you're there."

So, given the various distribution channels available to you from which to make your hotel choices, a good travel agent can certainly help you narrow your options. But beyond the matter of hotel selection, a great agent will have a relationship with the hotel management and can secure a more desirable room with a better layout and attractive view. A really great agent will negotiate special value-added components such as a room upgrade, spa treatment, gourmet meals, or limousine transport, at no additional cost to the traveler, along with prearrival arrangements to suit the traveler's preferences and needs—selected in-room beverages, publications, pillow type, dining reservations, and transfers.

Upchurch argues that you can sometimes find a cheaper option online to get a room at a desired hotel as opposed to going through a travel agent. "But what room have you purchased online?" he asks. "The small room that hasn't been renovated and shares a wall with the kitchen oven vent or the elevator shaft, with a view of a brick wall or parking lot? Most of the time, good travel agents have access to the same value-rates that can be found online, but a knowledgeable agent goes the extra mile to make sure the room you think you're reserving is the room that you'll experience upon arrival."

To be sure, matching an individual with the ideal hotel and guest room within that hotel is an art form, one that requires firsthand knowledge and insider connections. Hotels have personalities and styles that must complement those of the guests in order for a satisfying experience to transpire.

Other trends are having an impact on the selection of hotels by travelers and agents. Chain branding has evolved strongly over the past couple decades. Savvy travelers are learning what to expect from a Ritz-Carlton, Four Seasons, Mandarin Oriental, St. Regis, Orient Express, or Peninsula. But even these top hotel brands deliver a wide variety of styles and experiences within their respective hotel groups. For instance, the new Mandarin Oriental in Miami is vastly different from the Mandarin Oriental in Hong Kong—both are remarkable hotels, but one is ultracontemporary and the other is more traditional. So even with the onslaught of brand positioning, Virtuoso's Upchurch argues—not surprisingly—that travelers still need knowledgeable agents to explain the nuances in hotel selection.

Another trend that will further strengthen the value of a good travel consultant is the growth in popularity of boutique hotels, those with a smaller number of rooms and a distinct personality. These jewel properties are opening around the world, and they've been very well received by guests seeking a more intimate experience and personal recognition. Even Ritz-Carlton is launching a group of boutique hotels under the Bulgari name. Keeping track of these smaller, unique hotels will make the role of the travel agent that much more valuable to the traveler.

How do travel agents keep up with all this detailed information and all these personal contacts? Many agents have chosen to specialize in a particular destination or type of travel. For instance, if you want to go to Istanbul, you may be best served by a travel consultant who specializes in Turkey, and Istanbul in particular. When an agent decides to specialize in a destination, it usually means that the chosen destination is his or her passion, and that's great for the traveler. No one knows a destination and its lodging, dining, and recreational options like a true specialist, and no one is better connected with key contacts at the destination.

Beyond being a specialist, a travel agent can negotiate the best value for a traveler if he or she is part of a larger network and can flex the muscle and influence of a large combined buying power. For example, Virtuoso travel consultants have a combined annual buying power of more than $2.5 billion, and they can use that influence to negotiate the best values, amenities, and upgrades.

Why do hotel executives continue to cater to the travel agent community? It's simple: happy guests are more likely to become return guests, and they're more likely to refer their friends and colleagues. By working with top travel agents and taking the time to fully educate them on all aspects of the property, along with being honest with them about any challenges that exist, a hotel has the best chance of attracting clients that are the right fit for the experience provided, which ultimately gives the hotel and the agent the best chance of having satisfied guests and clients. Basically, top agents are savvy sales force extensions, and they're not paid (via commission) unless they make sales, so it remains a very attractive business model for premium and luxury hotels.

All in all, the selection of a hotel comes down to accountability. If you rely on a good travel agent to handle your travel planning and reservations, you have someone to turn to if any problem arises—someone who can correct the situation immediately. However, the ability to get such problems resolved often depends on price point. Below a certain price point—about $150 a night—most of us have diminished expectations for our hotel. Above that price point, the accountability factor weighs in.

The arguments for using the services of a great travel agent aren't new. For example, all of us can go to a well-stocked grocery store and buy the ingredients for a superb meal, but few of us can orchestrate those ingredients to create a true gourmet meal. A top travel consultant is like a chef who knows exactly which travel elements to combine to create a rewarding and memorable experience that perfectly matches and exceeds the expectations of the client. If you don't appreciate the skill required to achieve that, try making your own beef Wellington sometime—or arranging your own vacation itinerary. If you're like me, you'll be much happier relying on an expert in either scenario.

And within the travel agent community there are a number of other "elite" agent clubs—designed by the suppliers themselves—to create specialists. There are groups ranging from the Aruba Certified Expert program to "Aussie specialist" programs. And, yes, there's even a College of Disney Knowledge for travel agents. Most of these destination specialist programs are obviously geared toward motivating the travel agent as seller, but then what motivates you as a buyer are information and choice—and chances are better with one of these specialists that you'll get both.

But before you book with a travel agent, you should also consider this issue in terms of the agent's relationship with a hotel or resort. Many travel agents receive commissions not just on the room you book (and the rate you pay) but on the entire portfolio, which means they get a percentage in the form of a commission on anything you do at the hotel, whether it's dining at the hotel restaurant, using the spa, or playing nine holes on the golf course.

A preferred supplier relationship between the travel agent and the hotel may, in fact, get you a better room, and sometimes even a better rate, but you have an additional negotiating position here in the form of a rebate directly to you. Most agents would rather I not tell you this, for obvious reasons. But keep in mind that there is always room to negotiate, even with your travel agent.

Indeed, we live in a world of specialization. And Virtuoso remains my favorite consortium of expert travel agents.

SHOPPING THE INTERNET

The issue always comes down to price. Enter the explosive world of the Internet—and "explosive" may even be an understatement. The Internet has revolutionized not only the way we research hotel rooms but also the way we purchase them. It is a brave new world, and for people who know how to play the Internet game, the buyer's market is definitely your friend. But before you go shopping for discounts across the board, you need to consider these incontrovertible hotel finance facts.

Hotels can't make it on their room rates anymore. One reason is that some hoteliers simply spent too much money to either build, buy, or renovate their properties. Consider the venerable Clift Hotel in San Francisco, which recently filed for Chapter 11 bankruptcy protection from its creditors. Historically, a room at the Clift was always expensive—as far back as 1915 when it was a private hotel, then when it was one of the Four Seasons hotels, and recently when it was purchased and renovated by Ian Schrager. But the new incarnation of the Clift happened at a time of major hotel developments in San Francisco, the dot-com meltdown, a sagging economy, and the fear of travel fallout from the events of September 11, 2001.

Schrager spent $80 million to buy the place and another $50

million for a major renovation. Journalist Chris Barnett did the math: at 373 rooms, that meant an investment of $348,525 per room. Based on traditional amortization and debt service formulas, the hotel should be charging $350 per night for a room. But these days in San Francisco—and in so many other cities—supply is greatly outdistancing demand. Rates are depressed. And lately, a room at the Clift runs about $175. Perhaps that's why the bar there charges $11 for a mojito.

Can the Clift survive? Perhaps, but it's entirely possible that someone else may enter the picture, buy the hotel at a bargain price, charging about the same rate for rooms, and actually make a profit. This was clearly the case in the 1980s when Japanese investors spent huge sums of money to buy hotels that would never make a profit, given their purchase price. The Hyatt Waikoloa on the big island of Hawaii was built for something like $350 million. From almost the start, the hotel could not meet its debt service. Ultimately, the hotel was sold to Hilton for $90 million, and three months later, while actually charging less for rooms, the hotel was operating in the black. Hilton was able to lower the rates and still make money because the debt had been considerably diminished.

On the one hand, hotels are doing everything they can to cut back costs. On the other hand, their room rates have never been lower. This is where the Internet comes into play.

Let's continue with the premise that everything in travel is negotiable. A hotel deal offered by a travel agent, especially one with a preferred supplier relationship with the hotel, is negotiable beyond the initial offer. So are most deals offered on the Internet—and in many cases, Internet deals can be negotiated way beyond the initial offer. But before finding out how to pull that off, you need some history.

The Internet could be the single most powerful tool for smart travelers. It can also be a trap. The numbers are both seductive and daunting. The amount of online leisure and business travel booked without a travel agent grew a whopping 37 percent to $28 billion in 2002. To put that in perspective, 15 percent of all travel in 2002 was booked online. As you are reading this, global online travel sales are expected to reach $80 billion. PhoCusWright, which tracks the travel industry, estimates that hotel bookings online will increase from 9 percent of total gross bookings to one in five (20 percent) in the next year or so.

What this means is that some ninety-six million of us are now using the Internet for our travel needs, compared to twelve million in 1997. But is that necessarily a good thing? The answer is no.

The Internet is certainly a solution for many people who are looking for low airfares. But it is not always *the* answer when it comes to booking a hotel room.

As I've mentioned, it makes no sense to call a hotel's toll free number to make a reservation, because you almost always are directed to a clearinghouse that sells rooms at the highest possible rates with no room for negotiation. The call may be free, but you pay way too much for your room. Instead, I suggested that you call the hotel directly, speak to the manager on duty or the director of sales, people who can act as arbiters of their own inventory. They know, to a room, what the hotel's occupancy really is and are in the best position to negotiate, since an ironclad rule of the hotel business is that an unsold room is revenue a hotel can never recoup once the sun rises.

With the advent of the Internet, many travelers chose the expediency of making online hotel reservations, browsing for the best deals among various websites. Shopping on the Web is an excellent idea, but buying there can be another potential problem. So I still recommend that you deal with hotels to make reservations. Shop first on the Internet, get your calculator out, and then call the hotel directly. You may think that's too time consuming, but it could save you a lot of money. And in many cases, it also allows the hotel to earn more from renting you a room.

THIRD-PARTY WEBSITES

The original rationale for websites to market rooms for hotels was that this practice would help the hotels sell distressed inventory—that is, rooms that would otherwise go unsold. The situation was complicated with the entry of opaque websites, such as Hotwire and Priceline, that allowed many hotels to practice what amounted to plausible deniability with their parent corporations: a hotel could officially publish a certain rate and even post that rate on its own proprietary website, then dump excess rooms on the discount market. Initially, and at least on paper, this represented a win-win situation for the hotels and the websites. But the growth of third-party Internet booking sites has made managing hotel rates and inventory nearly impossible for many hotels, which means that it may not be a winning situation for anyone but the websites themselves.

For example, one major hotel in St. Louis faced an embarrassing excess of empty rooms. The hotel normally rented these rooms for as low as $139 per night. At the same time, the hotel's management estimated that it was costing $23 per day to service each room, rented or not. So it unloaded the excess rooms to one opaque website for $37, with the argument that some revenue, however small, was better than none at all.

The website, in turn, marked up the room to $89—$50 less than the official hotel rate. Travelers were happy, because they saved $50 per night. On paper, the hotel was happy because it didn't lose money. Or did it?

The websites undeniably sold many of those rooms that would otherwise have gone unoccupied. But as travelers discovered this new electronic distribution channel, an increasing number chose to use *only* the websites to book rooms, and, as a result, hotels started discounting a lot of rooms they didn't really need to discount. Their inventory of rooms wasn't really distressed to that degree. The demand curve was actually inelastic—when hotels lowered their prices, they also lowered their revenue. In the meantime, smart travelers who could do the math simply split the difference and were even happier. They called a hotel directly and made an offer—in this example, $59 a night. The hotel had good reason to agree to this. Under the original Web deal, it would earn just $37, while the website would make $52 more. When travelers called the hotel directly and negotiated, they saved $80 a night and the hotel made $22 more than if it had done the Web deal—a more satisfactory situation all around.

Many third-party websites, such as Expedia, Travelocity, or Hotels.com, mark up hotel rooms between 24 and 40 percent above the net rate the hotel gives them. That's huge. How huge? It wasn't that long ago that hotels used to complain about paying travel agent commissions. The third-party websites can actually triple that amount in markup.) But wait—the deal gets even sweeter for the third-party websites. These Internet sites charge local taxes on the sell rate, then they add a service charge. They pay the hotel the net rate they originally negotiated, as well as the tax on the net rate, but they pocket the tax and service charge on the difference between the net rate and the marked-up portion of the sell rate to the customer.

For example, a hotel gives website A a net rate of $100. The website agrees to pay the hotel $100 plus applicable taxes for every room it sells. Let's say the tax is 12.45 percent and the website charges you $150 to rent that room, which the hotel normally rents for $180. Based on this formula, the website sends the hotel a check for $112.45. But since they charged you $150 for the room plus $18.68 in tax (12.45 percent of $150) plus their service charge, the website nets $50 plus $6.23 for the difference between the tax charged to the customer and the tax paid to the hotel, plus the amount of the service charge. It's an advantageous profit position for them, and it results in lost tax revenues for cities and states. But the real bottom line is that you actually paid more than you needed to for that room.

Now let's apply this formula to the bigger picture. A major hotel getting business from the Internet could easily sell fifty-five thousand room-nights per year. If you calculate the markup and what these websites charge for taxes they aren't really collecting, the result represents a $250,000 money shift and lost tax revenues.

From a consumer perspective, at least in the short term, this is great news for travelers. If you know the average website markup (and now you know because I told you), simply call the hotel directly and split the difference between the net rate the hotel gave the website and the rate the website is charging. In most cases, the hotel is willing to negotiate a deal like this. It's a win-win proposition: more money for them, less money out of your pocket.

INTERNET LOW-RATE GUARANTEES

Website low-rate guarantees have to do with so-called rate integrity, which is probably as oxymoronic as the terms "postal service" and "airline food."

The aim of every hotel is to post a room rate and then stick to that rate. But I haven't found a hotel yet that's able to hold its rates, except during the peak holiday periods, especially with multiple distribution channels competing in a travel market directed by, if not frequently dominated by, the Internet. This is problematic for hotels. A recent survey by the Center for Hospitality Research at Cornell University revealed that hotels won't increase their revenue by discounting rates during slow economic times because consumers have learned to use the Internet to find discounts on rooms they intended to purchase anyway.

Virtually every hotel website, whether it is owned by the hotel corporation itself (Hilton, Hyatt, InterContinental) or is a third-party website, "guarantees" that it offers the lowest hotel room rates. That frequently turns out to be inaccurate. For example, Hotels.com advertises "up to 70% off hotel rooms," and that it has the lowest rates, "guaranteed." In actuality, however, in almost every hotel rooms are priced daily based on demand as measured by extremely sophisticated yield management software, and there are no longer official "rack rates" to discount from. There is no real discounting because pricing is set daily or even more frequently during the day. The competition in the marketplace dictates prices, and third-party websites like Hotels.com create an open view to all properties on the website, thereby causing downward pressure on prices.

Further, when a room at a hotel is priced very low on Hotels.com, it is likely that a traveler who reserves it will end up with the least desirable room in the hotel—it's the equivalent of that pair of four-inch red stilettos left over from the previous Christmas shopping season that is marked way down by midsummer.

Only the opaque websites consistently offer better prices than anyone else, but then the consumer has no control over the value of the purchase—in essence, trading need-to-know information for price. Sometimes you luck out and get a good value; the rest of the time you can end up in a disappointing mess. Hoteliers are selling their remaining inventory at the last minute for whatever they can get. Many try only to cover the cost of cleaning the room plus $5 or so. (Remember the St. Louis hotel and its $23 net rate?)

The use of the websites has grown so fast—exponentially, in fact—that it caught a lot of mainstream hotel chains off guard. As a result, more and more hotels began to lose control of their own inventory. A real battle ensued between the major chain hotel groups and their own franchisees. The chains insisted on retaining officially posted room rates, but the franchisees argued that they couldn't sell rooms at those rates and needed to get heads in beds at any price.

As the battle continues, the major hotel brands have gotten tough on their individual properties. Chains like InterContinental and Marriott are promising their guests the lowest rates on their own websites. Philip Wolf, president and CEO of Pho-CusWright, reports that "Best Western, the world's largest lodging franchise brand, now perceives Expedia . . . as a competitor in many cases, rather than a partner." Because of that dramatic relationship change, the major hotel chains are now requiring their individual properties to offer only those rates offered by the chains' own websites or be financially penalized. In some cases, they even lose their franchises.

Some hotels are playing even fiercer hardball. Hilton announced that anyone who booked a room on a travel website not affiliated directly with Hilton would not get frequent-stay points. In fact, some of the big chains have banded together to start their own website, Travelweb.com.

But has any of this put a stop to discounting? Of course not. Many franchises continue to turn to the opaque websites, which allow them that plausible deniability with their head offices. They can officially post rates on the main proprietary sites, yet still offer discount rates via opaque sites.

This may explain why Interactive Corporation, the parent of Expedia, just bought Hotwire.com, an opaque site, for $665 million in cash. To put things in perspective, that purchase amount is about a hundred times the total net profit that Hotwire has produced in its short existence. But look at some other numbers: Hotwire is selling seventy thousand rooms a week; Priceline sells one hundred thousand; Expedia and Travelocity sell more than that. And for the moment, those sales figures are only growing.

NAVIGATING THIS TANGLED WEB

Now that you have some background on the room pricing situation and the Internet's effect on it, how do you navigate this electronic war zone? My advice is: get ready to rumble!

Because the major hotel chains are so keen on controlling their inventory these days—it costs them 8 to 10 percent to book a room on their own websites versus 18 to 25 percent on other sites—you should always check with them first. After all, they are the primary suppliers. All too often, the discount websites prove to be more expensive, despite their low-price "guarantee."

I performed the following online check at three different websites: Hotels.com, Expedia, and the hotel's own website for the Holiday Inn Express in Tampa, Florida. In search of a regular room, I logged on to each site and checked the quotes for a two-night stay. Hotels.com listed the room at $71.95 per night, but the site added taxes and service charges of 12.78 percent, and the total for two nights came to $165. Expedia listed the same room at $74 a night, added 15.06 percent in taxes and service charges, and the total came to $170.30. On the Holiday Inn site, the room was listed at $68.97 per night. The site charged only a 12 percent room tax (what the city was charging), and the total came to $154.49.

Was this merely an exception? Hardly. I then checked out the Crowne Plaza Hotel at the San Francisco International Airport. For another two-night stay, Expedia showed a regular room at $119; with service charges and tax, the total came to $272.96. Hotels.com showed the room at $119.95, and the total with tax and service charges came to $281. On the Crowne Plaza website, the room listed at just $89, and only a 10 percent tax was charged, for a total of just $195.80—a whopping $85.20 less than the same room from Hotels.com, the site that "guarantees" the lowest rates!

In my search, I found only one deal where Hotels.com actually beat the rate offered by the hotel's own website: at another Crowne Plaza Hotel in Atlanta. How did that happen? Six Continents, the parent corporation of Crowne Plaza, explained that rooms are allocated to Hotels.com but not accessed electronically. When the hotel's prices change upward, it is the hotel's responsibility to check the third-party websites to ensure that the rates are in sync. In this case, they were not (another reason it pays to compare). Six Continents provides its hotels with specific instructions to set their Hotels.com price *the same as* their Internet rate to prevent the two from ever being reversed. But not every hotel stays on top of these rate fluctuations—and that's when consumers can benefit.

Now comes the fun part. You now know that sites like Expedia generally mark up their rooms 30 to 40 percent over the net rate they get from the hotels. They also charge hotels more for putting them on the first two pages of the website display. From the Tampa example, you can estimate that Expedia paid about $45 for the Holiday Inn Express room it was then selling on the Web for $74 (before service charges). You have nothing to lose by calling the hotel directly and offering to split the difference. Remember, anything you pay over $45 is money the hotel won't get from any other source. Again, you have nothing to lose by calling the hotel directly.

The moral of this story is that you should always check with the primary supplier. You'll be surprised how often you would pay a discounter more than if you went directly to the source.

Michael Shapiro, travel technology columnist for the *San Francisco Chronicle* and author of *Internet Travel Planner* (Globe Pequot, 2000), told me the following story. The sales director of an independent hotel in Kansas City recently e-mailed him that, at the time, the hotel's own Internet rate was $79 per night, compared with a "discount" rate of $129 from one of the giant online hotel sites. "During down times in our industry," he wrote, "especially for a small independent hotel, we're forced to sacrifice our rate in order to take advantage of the online hotel brokers' perception of a good deal. In fact, on most nights, we can offer a rate lower . . . through our own website or calling the hotel directly."

In 2003, JD Power and Associates released a survey showing that "guests who made reservations on the Internet in the mid-price and extended stay segments paid between two and five percent more than those who booked through traditional routes." Shapiro argues (and I wholeheartedly agree) that any agency, online or off, can call itself a "discount" agency and shout about its "discount" prices regardless of what it actually charges. There's nobody to hold any agency accountable for such claims, no matter how inaccurate they might be.

Does that mean you should avoid sites like Expedia and Hotels.com entirely? No. Because as the major hotels become more aggressive in trying to hold their prices, third-party websites will have to go the bundling route—offering deals on hotel rooms that include value-added extras such as rental cars and airfare. These websites also generally provide extremely useful search engines and geographical locators.

Of course, if you're willing to roll the dice, the opaque websites—where you really don't know where you're staying until you commit to a specific price—will continue to grow in popularity. One reason for this is that as the large hotel chains crack down on their franchisees, hotels using these sites remain exempt from the mandate or guarantee to match the room rate because consumers don't find out the name of the hotel they've booked until after they've made a nonrefundable buy.

There are other options, however. In addition to offering traditional air travel, most major U.S. airlines have increasingly begun to focus on combining flights with hotel stays and other perks to create bundled air-and-hotel vacation packages. These packages can mean one-stop shopping for travelers. But are they always the best deal? Let the buyer beware. On the United site, for example, the term "run of house" is used to describe some of the hotel choices. What this means is that the hotel can assign you to any room, on any floor it chooses—not always the best way to go.

Every once in a while, though, deals bundling airfare and hotels provide a great option. Michael Shapiro recently compared prices to three very different destinations (Jamaica, Hawaii, and the Netherlands) and then tracked departures in several different travel periods to avoid skewing the prices with advance-purchase requirements. He also selected sample rates for Monday, Wednesday, and Friday departures from the same gateway cities. These sample vacations consisted of three-, five-, and seven-night packages with comparable accommodations. Finally, for comparison purposes, he factored all taxes and fees for air travel into the prices.

His research revealed that, by and large, Expedia, Orbitz, and Travelocity each offer consistently lower prices than the airlines for comparable vacation packages. For example, for travel to Montego Bay, Jamaica, the three agencies' average low price for a three-night air-and-hotel vacation was $453 per person. For exactly the same vacation, using the same departure date, the four airlines that had availability had an average price of $877, a full $424 higher than the average from the big-three agencies.

The same trend held true in his Hawaiian vacation test. The sample starting rates he found for five-night packages from Los Angeles to Kauai were as low as $598 from Travelocity (with an average agency price of just $626), while the airlines, despite United's modest $647 price tag, had an overall average of $1,168, or $542 higher than the agency average.

Interestingly, Expedia had the best rates to both Amsterdam and Jamaica, and was close to the best price for Hawaii vacation packages. According to Teri Franklin, a product manager for Expedia, the agency's 11,000 Expedia Special Rate (ESR) hotel properties worldwide greatly contribute to the low prices. Expedia negotiates directly with the ESRs and can then pass on its savings to travelers. The value improves when the hotel rate is combined with airfare into a vacation package. Franklin says that packages tend to be less expensive than airfare and accommodations purchased separately because hotels can sell their rooms to a travel agency at lower prices than they feel comfortable posting publicly.

Shapiro notes, "The price disparity between the airlines and the agencies may be due to the fact that the airlines are limited to offering their own flights, or those of a codeshare partner, while an agency such as Travelocity can offer flights on hundreds of carriers."

One of my favorites, Site59.com, is a great place to find last-minute bundling deals on airfare and hotels. Not long ago, I needed to fly one of my researchers to Los Angeles on short notice. The cheapest deal—the least expensive walkup fare I could find anywhere—was $598 ($299 each way). But on Site59.com, I got a $436 deal, including round-trip airfare *and* a four-star hotel in L.A. that I didn't even need.

 THREE USEFUL WEBSITES (WITH APPROPRIATE CAUTIONS)

- www.all-hotels.com: A U.K.-based website with more than seventy-seven thousand properties. Not always the best prices, but a good place to start if you're heading overseas.
- www.luxres.com: Looking for upscale four- and five-star hotels? This is the place to start—at least for information.
- www.quikbook.com: This site doesn't have the biggest online hotel listings, but I like that the site doesn't charge a booking fee.

The future of travel distribution channels, at least in the short term, could very well be the opaque websites. This provides the individual hotels a shield from the rate mandates of their corporate management. And if you play the game well, it lets you, the consumer, win as well.

However, the landscape of opaque websites can be tricky. With Priceline.com, for example, assuming you've done your homework and know about what the market will bear for a hotel room in a certain location at a certain hotel, you place your bid. But there are no assumptions that your offer will be accepted— and under the current Priceline system, if your offer is rejected, you must wait three days for another opportunity to place a free bid again for that same room. Ah, but clever Priceline players know there's a loophole in the system. It's known as "using non-four-star zones," and it allows you to rebid almost immediately.

Here's how it works. You've placed your bid for a four-star hotel on Priceline, and it's been rejected. Priceline allows you to rebid only if you substantially increase your bid and meet a few other requirements. But Priceline also requires you to pick another area of town, lower your requirements (go down a star or two), and/or change the dates of your intended stay.

Here's the secret for free rebidding. Not all locations (zones) in the Priceline inventory have hotels in every quality category. Returning to our example, you've been rejected on your bid for the four-star hotel in a particular zone. So simply find another zone in the same city that doesn't have any four-star properties and slightly raise your bid price.

When you add a new zone to your second bid attempt, it qualifies you for the free rebid that Priceline offers. Here's the cool part: since the new zone you're choosing doesn't contain any four-star hotels, you won't be stuck with a hotel in that zone, and you can rebid for your original hotel.

If you can find a lower rate on some sites, such as Hotels. com, you also need to be responsible for confirming that reservation as well as the rate, even if you get an e-mail from the website telling you it's a done deal. Why? Here's a little-known fact, which continues to astound me. When you make a reservation on a site like Hotels.com, the site may confirm the deal with you by e-mail, but it sends the reservation to the hotel involved by fax! It seems absurd, but it happens—and this is where the chain of information can break down. I don't depend on my *own* fax machine; why would I want to depend on someone else's? Once you get that e-mail confirmation, call the hotel directly to confirm it. One of my sources tells me that about 7 percent of the faxed confirmations are never received by the hotels. That is just not an acceptable average.

Michael Shapiro offers a few other rules of the road for navigating the Internet in search of travel deals:

- Some third-party websites list hotels as sold out only because their allotment of rooms at the proprietary rate is sold out. There may be plenty of rooms at that hotel, but if the website doesn't have them available at the special rate, they are listed as sold out. This is a ploy to redirect consumers to other hotels with which the website has an arrangement.

- Check Orbitz, which uses a grid system where you can compare price versus star rankings. Keep in mind, though, that some of the star rankings are subjective.

- Check regional directories—for example, www.hotelres.com for San Francisco or Venere.com for some European countries.

- Try Hotwire and Priceline if you're flexible. Shapiro regards Hotwire and Priceline as much better for hotels than for flights. It's a big trade-off to be able to fly any time of day, but Shapiro says that if he can get a three-star hotel for $30, then he doesn't care whether it's a Holiday Inn or a Quality Inn. In places like San Francisco where occupancy has been low, you can book beautiful hotels such as the Hyatt Regency through Priceline for under $40. Check Biddingfortravel. com and Betterbidding.com to see what other people are paying.

Finally, follow the advice I gave you at the beginning of this chapter: always call the hotel directly and deal.

CHAPTER 3

The Truth about Stars and Diamonds

Although the travel industry may be price driven, total information is what travelers seek most immediately. They are desperate for facts about hotels—news they can use. This goes way beyond just price to include factors such as location, services, room design, safety, and security—as well as attitude.

LOST IN TRANSLATION

Many of us grew up looking at glossy hotel brochures and daydreaming about exotic locations. Some of us are still looking at those brochures. If we're honest, we'll admit to at least once having been seduced by the language used in them—superlatives like *best, greatest, finest,* and *most.* The brochure shows a happy couple walking hand in hand along the hotel's *most* beautiful beach. Ken and Barbie, in their tennis whites, volley on the *best* court. And the sun is always setting beautifully in the *finest* location. Get the picture? The problem, of course, is that the picture is too often grossly misleading.

These deceptive images appear not only in brochures, but also on many websites. Often, websites are nothing more than electronic brochures and are driven more by transactional pressures than by a desire to be impartially informational.

There are some additional danger words. One of the funniest glossaries I've ever read (keeping in mind the element of truth in humor) was written a number of years ago by Denver innkeeper Charles Hillestad. Here's his list of misleading phrases commonly used in hotel and B&B brochures. Keep the real meanings of these words and phrases in mind the next time you are looking to book a hotel room.

Commonly Used Phrases	What They Really Mean
Rustic	The plumbing is out back.
Quaint	Bare lightbulbs dangle from the ceiling.
Romantic	No electricity at all; candles required.
Cozy	Your suitcase has more square footage than your room.
Invigorating	No elevators.
Memorable	Pet boa constrictor occasionally escapes.
Antiques	Used furniture.
Relaxing	Nothing to do.
Endearing	Beds littered with stuffed teddy bears, pigs, geese, or unicorns.
Friendly	Innkeeper smiles when pocketing your check.
Professional	Innkeeper wears shoes and shirt.
Cultured	Innkeeper knows Vivaldi is not a sports car.
Elegant	Even the venetian blinds have tassels.
Plush	Only three towels are needed to dry your hands (too bad there are only two).
Luxurious	Towels will actually fit around your waist.
Original	Unpainted.
Once in a lifetime	No one ever returns.
Inspected	In 1942.
Newly refurbished	In 1942.
Authentic	Couldn't afford to rip out and replace.

Accessible	By military vehicles with metal tracks.
Historic	Built prior to George W. Bush's inauguration.
Lodge	Anything built of logs with the bark still on.
Suite	Any room larger than the bed.
Bridal suite	Any room with a four-poster bed.
Free-spirited	Bathing suits are optional in the hot tub.
Healthy	Tofu served for breakfast and high tea.
Mountain view	The calendar photo on the wall.
Garret	A place to bump your head.
Wooded acreage	More than one tree.
Within walking distance	Within driving distance.
Within driving distance	No more than a short plane ride.
Amenities	Soap provided.
Entertainment	Innkeeper's daughter plays accordion.
Smoking prohibited	You will be frisked upon arrival.
Smoking discouraged	Unless you have money.
Continental breakfast	Coffee and yesterday's Danish.
Extended Continental breakfast	Coffee, orange-colored juice, and *choice* of yesterday's Danish.
Air-conditioned	Windowpanes broken.
Recommended	Innkeeper's mother likes the place.
Approved	Innkeeper's father likes the place.
Inn	Hotel, motel, home stay, restaurant, or anything at all with rooms.
Country inn	An inn located anywhere, including downtown.

We really can't—nor should we—depend on brochures, whether traditional or electronic, for anything other than a hotel's phone number and address. Recently I logged on to the website for a small hotel in New Orleans. Based on what I read there, when you stay at this hotel you feel "as though you're a French aristocrat in the Victorian era . . . greeted with warm southern hospitality and shown to your room where you can relax from your trip surrounded by authentic Victorian furniture." Can you suspend your disbelief long enough to consider booking a room at this place?

SEEING STARS AND DIAMONDS

When all is said and done, the defining factor in choosing a hotel is service. But how do you measure service? The United States has no standardized, national system of rating hotels, however, dozens of companies rate hotels here. The two most prominent companies are the American Automobile Association (AAA) and Mobil, both of which publish ratings books. In the hotel business, a five-star or five-diamond rating is the equivalent of an Academy Award because of the visibility that comes with this level of recognition. These rating systems are helpful to a degree, but if a hotel claims a high rating, always ask who did the evaluating.

AAA Diamond Ratings

The AAA evaluations are based on twenty-seven diamond rating requirements covering the hotel's exterior, grounds and public areas, bathrooms, housekeeping and maintenance, room decor, management, and guest services. A hotel is awarded one to five diamonds according to its evaluation results.

- *One diamond:* No frills, but basic requirements are met with comfort, cleanliness, and hospitality.

- *Two diamonds:*   Modest accommodations at a moderate price.

- *Three diamonds:*   Multifaceted properties with more style, and upgrades of physical attributes, amenities, and comfort.

- *Four diamonds:*   Upscale in all categories, with a higher degree of hospitality, service, and attention to detail.

- *Five diamonds:*   "The ultimate in luxury and sophistication."

In the 2003 AAA guidebooks, 6.4 percent of hotels rate one diamond and 34 percent rate two diamonds. The majority— 53.8 percent—are three-diamond properties, while only 2.8 percent rate four diamonds and a mere 0.2 percent are five-diamond hotels. The AAA guidebooks are free to members.

AAA claims that it employs approximately eighty full-time inspectors who visit more than thirty thousand hotels and motels each year. Many of these inspectors spend more than two hundred nights per year in hotels. AAA inspectors run down a thorough checklist at each property. For a hotel to get at least one diamond, certain nonnegotiable criteria must be met, ranging from how many hangers are in the closets to how many sinks are in the bathroom. Approximately 6 percent of all lodgings that are inspected each year fail to meet AAA minimum rating requirements.

Mobil Star Ratings

Mobil star ratings, launched in 1958, are similar to AAA's diamond ratings in meaning and impact, although the Mobil approach to determining the ratings is somewhat different. The bar is set by the hoteliers and restaurateurs themselves, and the criteria concern physical facilities and services you are likely to find beyond a certain price point. There are forty thousand hotels in the United States but only five thousand get any star rating at all from the Mobil guidebooks, which are sold to the public.

Mobil conducts both announced physical inspections and unannounced visits. On the physical inspections, Mobil staffers, including some part-time inspectors and contract personnel, perform exhaustive and anonymous evaluations. The detailed facilities review includes four hundred questions that can be answered only by yes or no. In addition, there are quality assurance evaluations that focus on the overall guest experience. Mobil inspectors have been known to use stopwatches to time the delivery of services. They also evaluate the level of courtesy with which these services are delivered. These basics constitute 35 percent of the overall inspections.

Seconds count. To qualify for a Mobil four-star rating, the registration process must take less than three minutes and forty-eight seconds; for a five-star rating, it must take less than three minutes and twenty seconds. The maximum time allowed for baggage to get to a room is ten minutes and fifteen seconds for a four-star rating and seven minutes and twenty-three seconds for a five-star rating. Some inspectors will intentionally remove lightbulbs from lamps to see how long it takes the hotel to notice and correct the deficiency.

Occasionally someone will tip off a hotel that an inspector is about to check in. Hotels will go to extreme lengths—everything short of sending in a biohazard team to sterilize a room—if they suspect that a AAA or Mobil inspector is about to arrive. And once in a while, the hotel actually has a sense of humor about it. One inspector checked into a hotel room in a southern state and immediately thought something might be up. His suspicions were confirmed when he did his obligatory under-the-bed check, where he spied a piece of paper. He reached in, pulled it out, and read: "Yes, we even cleaned under here!"

One AAA inspector was staying at a hotel in North Carolina that was advertising a special $24.95 rate. As the inspector stood at the front desk completing his registration form, two senior citizens came in and asked about a room. The clerk told them the rate. But then one of the prospective guests opened his wallet and took out his AAA card, his AARP card, and a Days Inn Senior Discount card. Without hesitation, the clerk smiled, reached in his pocket, pulled out a $5 and two $1 bills, and placed them under the room key. "Sir, if you want me to honor all those dis-

CONFESSIONS OF THE HOTEL INSPECTORS:

Here are some true tales from the AAA inspector files:

A campground had requested that it be inspected for possible listing in a particular guidebook. It turned out to be a nudist camp. The manager met the inspector at his car and stood there, in the buff, trying to defend why it should be acceptable to list his property. The campground never did get listed.

A tourism editor had stopped to inspect a motel in southern Mississippi, when a couple of AAA members walked in. "Apparently they had just stopped at a small place up the road—not an AAA-listed property," he reported. "They said that when they got to their room, everything was filthy: the sheets were dirty, the wastebasket was full, and the bathroom hadn't yet been cleaned. The members assumed the maid just hadn't gotten there yet, but after some time had passed, they called the front desk to inquire. "Oh yeah," the fellow said. "If you want your room cleaned, that's five dollars extra!"

counts, I'm going to owe *you* money!" the clerk quipped. This exchange registered with the inspector, who awarded a higher rating to the hotel.

RATING THE RATINGS

The bottom line is that, as detailed as these rating systems might be, they are still subjective. For example, when it opened more than ten years ago, the upscale Lanesborough Hotel in London announced it was the city's only six-star hotel. How did that happen? The hotel awarded all six stars—to itself! The Scottish press recently reported that one new hotel would become Scotland's only seven-star hotel. Recently, the over-the-top Burj al Arab Hotel in Dubai made a similar seven-star self-pronouncement.

The situation gets even worse, when you recognize that in some countries the star system is nothing more than an arbitrary government-issued designation for taxation purposes: the more stars in the rating, the higher the room price—and the more the government can tax. In fact, many hotels in Italy try to refuse additional stars in order to pay less tax.

Overseas, the star system is, at best, misleading from the get-go. In the United States, there's at least an attempt to match the level of quality, service, and design with the number of stars or diamonds awarded.

Occasionally, inspectors will discover a systemwide problem with hotels that they are able to change. In 1993, AAA began an intense lobbying campaign concerning hotel security. The goal was to arrive at better minimum standards for hotel guest security, and the focus was on door locks. Two years earlier, a AAA survey indicated that 90 percent of its members expected deadbolt locks in their hotel rooms, as well as between adjoining rooms. Consequently, AAA amended its ratings system to require dead-bolt locks on all guest room doors in order to even qualify for rating by the organization.

As I've mentioned, hotel managers will go to great lengths to rate that extra star or diamond, and losing a star or diamond is tantamount to catastrophe. The numbers, at least superficially, seem to justify that. There are approximately 36 million AAA members, and they travel. Annually, they spend more than 150 million room-nights in hotels.

Are you impressed? Yes, I admit those numbers seem impressive. But how important are the ratings? From a hotel's point of view, it's a major ego trip for the owner and management company to merit those extra diamonds or stars. It's likewise a great employee morale booster. Furthermore, from a bottom-line perspective, it allows the hotel to command and justify premium rates. But from the perspective of the traveler, these ratings systems may ultimately have far less of an impact on the quality of the experience and the satisfaction level than on the person's wallet. The star and diamond systems can be easily misconstrued, intentionally misplaced, or simply misunderstood.

The AAA rating decision at, for example, a thousand-room resort complex, with six separate food outlets and three golf courses, may be based on an inspector visit that lasts just half a day. If that hotel gets extra diamonds because it has a great designer golf course but you don't play golf, how does that translate into a five-diamond experience for you? It doesn't. But it certainly enables the hotel to charge higher rates. For many years, the old Desert Inn in Las Vegas maintained the highest average room rate on the Strip—all because it had a golf course that helped it earn a higher rating.

Do you really care if there are real, fresh flowers in the vase in your guest room if the hotel hasn't upgraded its fire safety system and could burn down at any moment? Your priorities and criteria for a hotel may differ from those of the AAA and Mobil inspectors. In fairness, both AAA and Mobil publish guidebooks, *not* bibles, and they should be used as such. I've found both useful, but neither is essential to my travel decisions.

DEVELOPING YOUR OWN RATING SYSTEM

What counts is keeping track of your own personal hotel experiences. In 2001, *Forbes* magazine polled its readers for personal accounts of their own hotel horror stories. One reader found a corpse under his bed in São Paolo. (I guess they didn't clean under *that* bed!) Another reader reported blood splatters in his hotel bathtub in Las Vegas, and a strange noise coming from between the boxspring and the mattress at a hotel in Cincinnati turned out to be a cat.

You need to develop your own set of criteria for what constitutes a great hotel experience. You won't be able to do this based on a single hotel stay or just by checking off a list. A workable system will be the culmination of your own personal hotel experiences and preferences. After a few stays at different hotels, I guarantee that you will start to develop your own star or diamond system.

As AAA and Mobil did, start with the basics: service, cleanliness, and safety. These are truly a matter of substance over style. I couldn't care less how many times an employee of a Ritz-Carlton responds to a guest's request by saying, "My pleasure" or "Certainly." What I *do* care about is that guest requests are handled quickly, quietly, and efficiently. Unless the request is illegal or immoral, hotel staff should reverse Nancy Reagan's famous dictum and "just say *yes*."

My suggestions for your own pre-check-in general rating system, in no particular order, are as follows:

- How accessible is the elevator from your room?

- How early will your room be available for you to check in?

- When is the real, drop-dead checkout time?

- How does the actual size of a standard room compare to that of a deluxe room?

- How close is the front desk to the hotel's entrance?

- Is the staff cross-trained? During peak check-in times, is there a long line in front of the check-in counter, while the cashier area is fully staffed and without lines? Conversely, during peak checkout times, is the front desk staff idle?

A few small observations can go a long way toward refining your personal rating system. For example, examine the elevators. Are the buttons scratched or the numbers worn off? Then take a closer look at the door tracks as the elevator door opens and closes on each floor. If each of those floors is regularly cleaned, the door tracks will shine all the way up.

I developed my never-fail hotel service test at the Ritz-Carlton in Laguna Niguel, California. I call it the Diet Coke test. (Of course, you can use any carbonated soft drink for this test.) If you're like me, you hate the taste of carbonated soft drinks that come from a bartender's "gun" dispenser. They always seem to be too carbonated or they have too much syrup, or you can taste other soft drinks in the mix. However, at most bars and restaurants, simply because of the higher profit margin, soft drinks come from the gun.

But this is not necessarily true at hotels—and here's where the test is useful. I entered the Ritz-Carlton and asked for a Diet Coke in a can or bottle. The waitress replied that this wasn't possible. *Wrong answer.* I then gently explained to her that it *was* possible: the hotel stocked cans and bottles for room service; there was even a vending machine for employees that dispensed cans or bottles of Diet Coke. The waitress was peeved, but I got the drink I wanted.

I had the opposite experience when I stayed at a Best Western on Prince Edward Island in Canada, where it was about five degrees below zero. I went into the only place open in town—the coffee shop at the hotel. The waitress asked what I wanted to drink, and I requested a Diet Coke in a bottle or can. "You wait right here, honey," she said. Without hesitation, she put on her coat, walked across a four-lane highway to a convenience store, and returned with a six-pack. "Figured you might want these for later," she commented. She remains my hero.

The Ritz-Carlton is a five-star, five-diamond property. The Best Western wasn't even rated by the guidebooks at that point. Nevertheless, it rates high with me. My guest room there had bad shag carpets and cinderblock walls; I'm convinced the television set gave off lethal doses of radiation. The fluorescent lights gave me a headache, and the bed sagged. But the superior service demonstrated by my Diet Coke experience would bring me back.

CHAPTER 4

Checking Out Before You Check In

The great advantage of a hotel is that it's a refuge from home life.

— *George Bernard Shaw*

Checking Out Before You Check In

After you've looked at all the brochures, read the guide-books and ratings books, and arrived at a price you feel comfortable paying, there are questions you need to ask that should ultimately determine your decision to stay at a particular hotel.

DEFINE YOUR TERMS

Each day the hotel industry sells 2.5 million rooms. If you are contemplating renting one of these rooms, then you first need to arrive at a mutually agreeable definition with the hotel of the actual type of room you're getting. Following are some commonly used definitions:

Single: A room with one double bed or one-person occupancy.

Double: A room with one double bed or two-person occupancy.

Queen: A room with a queen-size bed.

King: A room with a king-size bed.

Twin: A room with two (single or double) beds.

Double/double: A room with two double beds.

Parlor: A living or sitting room that isn't used as a bedroom (called a *salon* in some parts of Europe).

Suite: A parlor connected to one or more bedrooms.

Junior suite: A large room with a partition that separates the bedroom from the sitting area.

Duplex: A two-story suite in which the parlor and bedroom(s) are connected by a stairway.

Lanai: A room that overlooks water or a garden. Such rooms have a balcony or patio and are usually found in resort hotels.

Cabana: A room that is adjacent to the pool area. It may or may not have sleeping facilities. Such rooms are usually separate from the hotel's main building.

Efficiency: An accommodation that contains a kitchen facility.

Connecting rooms: Two or more rooms with private, connecting doors that permit access between the rooms without having to enter the corridor.

Adjoining rooms: Two rooms located side by side. Such rooms may or may not have a connecting door.

And then there's something called a "run of house" room. You definitely want to avoid that category, because it can mean any room the hotel wants to dump on you.

But that's just for starters. You also need to ask some questions about square footage. One Chicago hotel offers two types of rooms, "deluxe" and "superior." The only difference is about eight square feet; other than that, the rooms are essentially the same. This is a typical hotel trick used to drive up revenue from those who persist in thinking that being "upgraded" really justifies a higher rate. The guest pays $50 more and essentially gets nothing extra.

LOCATION, LOCATION, LOCATION

Once you've arrived at a mutually agreed-upon definition of the room you want, your next concern should be where the room is located. In my first Travel Detective book, I suggested that you ask the reservations desk, "How close is my room to the construction?"—the presumption being that at any given time every hotel is undergoing internal renovation somewhere. Obviously, you want to be as far away from that renovation work as possible, but since renovation is an ongoing process, you should also ask if the hotel can put you in one of their recently renovated rooms. If none exist, that's a huge red flag.

A hotel undergoing renovation is not necessarily a bad thing, especially if you are forewarned. In some cases, you can negotiate a precipitous drop in room rate by letting the hotel know that you are aware of the renovation process and you accept that the noise and inconvenience levels will be greater than normal. For example, some hotels actually publish renovation rates. On the big island of Hawaii, the Waikoloa Beach Marriott advertised "retrofit" rates during the installation of a new $600,000 automatic fire sprinkler system. The rooms were discounted 45 percent—an oceanfront room that normally went for $485 rented for $269.

Here is a politically incorrect hotel secret: if a hotel is not full, and you are not displacing a physically challenged person who needs the room, you can ask if there's a handicapped-accessible room available. This is not the same as arrogantly parking your car in a handicapped space, which is clearly wrong (not to mention illegal). Usually, these rooms are much larger than regular rooms and, even for those of us who are not physically challenged, they can be preferable to regular rooms because they are well-thought-out and practical in terms of both design and function.

If you value peace and quiet and your hotel typically caters to large conventions, ask on which floors the group(s) will be staying and then pick another floor to book your own room. Likewise, you don't want to book a guest room that is on the way to or from the snack area, sports center, or lounge.

You should also ask about other local events that could sabotage your stay. I made this mistake once at a hotel in Kyoto, Japan, where I neglected to ask what other events were scheduled at the hotel that would coincide with my stay there. By the time I arrived, it was too late. I was one of only about four other guests at this six-hundred-room hotel who were not attending any one of several different weddings being held that night or the next day. I'm not making this up: by the second afternoon, I had become so crazed by the nonstop celebrating that I actually attended one of the ceremonies—I really had no other choice.

Hotels will often set aside blocks of rooms for specific guests, but sometimes these blocks can be moved. Also, there is usually a showroom that is reserved for sales, but, in a pinch, it too can be made available to guests who ask. My theory is that getting a great room at a hotel your first time is usually a combination of luck and good timing. Getting a terrific room your second time is a combination of good planning and a phone call or two.

 QUESTIONS NOT TO ASK

The following are actual questions asked by hotel guests:

- "Is there somewhere I can buy this coffeemaker for my mom? If not, then I am just going to take it."
- "I am from Ohio and I am dying for a joint. Do you know where I can get one?"
- "Your rooms don't have water beds, do they? My wife gets seasick."
- "Did anyone walk out the front door lately?"
- "Do a lot of people steal towels? . . . I didn't."
- "I was calling to find out if you have any used sheets for sale."
- "Can I have ten rolls of toilet paper to TP a car in the parking lot?"

The best hotel in the world is the hotel you're best known in. Get to know the people who work at the hotel—the general manager, the sales manager, or key people at the front desk. On your next trip, make sure you book your reservations through them and that you confirm with them that you're coming.

A ROOM WITH A VIEW

How important is it to you to book a room with a view at a hotel? In my opinion, unless you have decided to literally move into the hotel, a room with a view is highly overrated, for a number of reasons. First, the higher the floor, the more time it will take you to leave the hotel—specifically, the elevator then becomes a local all the way down to the first floor (bring reading material). Second, it's no surprise that hotels price rooms with good views at a higher rate than they do other rooms.

The third and perhaps most important consideration is a safety issue. It is difficult, if not impossible, for most fire departments to get above the eighth floor in any building. If you're in a room with a great view on a high floor at a hotel, in the event of a fire you're guaranteed a spectacular view—of the fire department's futile efforts to reach you.

Nevertheless, if you insist on that great view and don't necessarily want to pay for it, follow this advice. It's logical to assume that every hotel's presidential suite has the best view. It also stands to reason that the suite frequently connects to a regular room. Furthermore, odds are excellent that the presidential suite is unoccupied more often than it is occupied. (The same usually applies to many of the larger suites at any hotel.) So when you are checking in, let the front desk clerk know that you don't want a suite but would be willing to rent one of the connecting rooms instead. You get the same great view, but at a substantially lower rate.

Note that I am urging you to be finicky when it comes to selecting a hotel room. Most good hotels will show you rooms before you register, and they will usually let you see more than one, so you can make your decision. At the Hyatt Regency in Maui, rooms with a view that face the pool are incredibly noisy because kids are in that pool yelling and screaming for hours. I always choose a room on the other side of the hotel, facing away from the water. Previewing the room choices can clue you in to situations like this.

Another good question to ask is whether your room is located over a loading bay. Noise in this part of a hotel often starts as early as 2 A.M., when the sanitary staff arrives to cart away the rubbish after a ballroom or banquet function. Especially at some city hotels, a room with a view can often be a problem due to noise from the street—or sometimes even from within the hotel itself.

Every hotel has rooms to avoid, for different reasons. So don't be afraid to be choosy. Avoid rooms near the bar at the National Hotel in Miami. At the Grande Bretagne in Athens, despite double-glazed windows, a room with a view means constant noise from cars and buses running around the square. I advise you to walk around and scout the layout when you first arrive at any new hotel. Only once you've done that should you check in.

BLOCKING

When you check into a hotel, you're always asked to present a credit card. Hotel clerks will tell you they want to make an imprint of the card. Yes, they are doing that—and much more.

The process is called *blocking*, and I warned about it in the first Travel Detective book. A few years ago this meant that if your hotel room cost $250 a night and you were staying five nights, the hotel could easily block charges of about $1,250, or five times the amount of your daily rate. Today some hotels actually will block ten times the amount of your daily rate to cover the room rate and anything else you might charge to your room. This protects the hotel and ensures that it gets paid. But if you're using a Visa, MasterCard, or Discover card when you check in—cards that have preset spending limits—the hotel might very easily have maxed out your available credit by blocking. What's worse, even if you never reach the total amount of blocked charges, it can take as many as ten business days for those charges to be reversed. Most hotels do not disclose this practice, and it becomes particularly embarrassing when you try to use your credit card and discover the charge has been denied because you're suddenly over your limit.

In a downward economy, as hotels struggle to generate as much revenue as possible, the problem of blocking has actually gotten worse. However, the solution remains the same: if at all possible, use an American Express or Diners Club card, which carries no preset spending limit, to check in, even if you have no intention of using that card to pay your bill upon checkout. Then, when you check out, ask the clerk to destroy the American Express or Diners Club imprint and present your Visa, MasterCard, or Discover card instead. If you don't carry an American Express or Diners Club card, ask the hotel to disclose to you upon check-in the amount of their blocking charge and request that they block only on a per-day basis rather than on a per-stay basis.

ROOM MIX

Another potential pitfall for travelers is something called the *room mix*. Some hotels like to maintain European-style occupancy, which means that rooms contain two twin beds instead of two full- or queen-size beds. This discourages an excessive number of people from staying in one hotel room because only one person can really fit in those small beds.

At most hotels, only one rollaway bed is permitted per room, as well. But here's a little trick that can save you money. If you ask for a rollaway bed for an adult many hotels will charge you, but if you ask for a rollaway bed for a child they won't. Guess what? Most rollaway beds are the exact same size.

It is much easier to rent a room with a king-size bed rather than a European twin. The twin-bed rooms and the smoking rooms are the least desirable rooms, so hotels try to push these rooms first. For example, the check-in clerk might tell you that the only available rooms at that time are smoking or twin and ask you whether you would like to wait until a nonsmoking room becomes available. The answer, unless you are totally desperate, is to wait.

WHEN IS A RESERVATION NOT A RESERVATION? (THE MYTH OF THE GUARANTEED ROOM)

> It is equally offensive to speed a guest who would like to stay and to detain one who is anxious to leave.
> — *Homer*

Let's assume you've done your homework, you've shopped the Internet, you've called the hotel directly, and you've asked all the pre-check-in questions. You're prepared to use the right credit card when you get to the front desk.

But eventually you will have to get *beyond* the front desk to your room—and therein lies a potential problem: just because you have a reservation doesn't mean you have a room.

The story goes like this. A man walks up to the front desk of a very popular, exclusive hotel and says he is there to check in, that he has a guaranteed reservation. The clerk checks and confirms the reservation but tells the man that the hotel is completely sold out and that there are no rooms available.

The man insists he has a reservation. The clerk insists there are no rooms.

Finally, frustrated and growing angrier by the moment, the would-be guest has an idea. "Let me ask you a question," he begins. "If the president of the United States arrived right now, would you have a room for him?"

The clerk thinks for just a moment and then replies, "Yes, sir, we would have a room for him."

"Well, guess what," the man laughs, "the president isn't showing up tonight, so I'll take *his* room!"

You may get a chuckle out of that story, but the awful truth remains that hotels often overbook. Although a reservation is, in fact, an implied contract and hotels are thus in potential breach of contract every time they overbook, most guests don't press the point.

To further complicate the situation, there is a long-standing hotel industry tradition that a reservation is held until 6 P.M. and then released. This convention is now being ignored by more and more hotels.

And there's something even worse: the myth of the guaranteed room. Most hotels in the United States offer the option of guaranteeing your room reservation with a credit card. At least in theory, this means that you've bought the room whether you show up or not, and, more important, no matter what time you show up, that room will be ready for you.

Not necessarily.

Some cases of overbooking have even ended up in court. Consider the recent and celebrated adventure of Tom Farmer. Al Capone once said that "you can get more with a nice word and a gun than you can with a nice word." In Tom Farmer's case, he got nowhere with the nice word, but when he used a gun—in this case, e-mail, he got everyone's attention.

After a long and arduous business trip (yes, his flight was delayed), Farmer and a colleague, Shane Atchison, both directors of ZAAZ, a Web design/technology consultancy in the Pacific Northwest, landed in Houston. It was 2 A.M. on November 15, 2001. Farmer had reserved a room earlier at the Houston DoubleTree—more than just reserved the room, he had guaranteed his reservation on his credit card. In addition, he was a Hilton HHonors club member and had already attained Gold VIP status.

Farmer arrived at the front desk exhausted and just hoping for about four hours' sleep in his guaranteed room before the next morning's business meeting. However, he hadn't counted on a confrontation with Mike.

Mike was working the front desk that night. Totally devoid of compassion or sympathy, night clerk Mike informed Farmer that the DoubleTree was overbooked and that his room had been given to someone else hours before.

Farmer's initial shock came from the fact that the hotel would give away a room that had been guaranteed by a credit card. Mike was indifferent to this. Farmer's shock was compounded when Mike didn't offer to find him another room elsewhere.

So Farmer decided to fight back—on the Internet. He and Shane sat down and composed an elaborate, hysterical, sarcastic, and downright wicked seventeen-page PowerPoint presentation and e-mailed it to the DoubleTree management. He also e-mailed a copy to the mother-in-law of one of his colleagues. Here is an excerpt from this presentation:

Yours Is a Very Bad Hotel

A graphic complaint prepared for:

Joseph Crosby
General Manager
Lisa Rinker
Front Desk Manager

DoubleTree Club Hotel
2828 Southwest Freeway
Houston, Texas

In the Early Morning Hours of November 15, 2001, at the DoubleTree Club Houston, We Were Treated Very Badly Indeed.

We are Tom Farmer and Shane Atchison of Seattle, Washington.
We held guaranteed, confirmed reservations at the DoubleTree Club for the night of November 14–15.
These rooms were held for late arrival with a major credit card.
Tom is a card-carrying Hilton HHonors Gold VIP . . .
Yet when we arrived at 2:00 A.M., we were refused rooms!
Refused rooms . . . even when we're "confirmed" and "guaranteed"?
Mike, your night clerk, said the only rooms left were off-limits because their plumbing and air-conditioning had broken!
He'd given away the last good rooms three hours ago!
He'd done nothing about finding us accommodation elsewhere!
And he was deeply unapologetic!

Quotations from Night Clerk Mike:

"Most of our guests don't arrive at two o'clock in the morning."
—2:08 A.M., November 15, 2001

Explaining why it was *our* fault that the DoubleTree Club could not honor our guaranteed reservation

We Discussed with Mike the Meaning of the Term "Guarantee."

guar·an·tee (ger-an-tē), *n.*

Something that assures a particular outcome or condition: Lack of interest is a guarantee of failure.

A promise or an assurance, especially one given in writing, that attests to the quality or durability of a product or service.

A pledge that something will be performed in a specified manner.

Mike Didn't Much Care.
He seemed to have been betting that we wouldn't show up. When we suggested that the least he should have done was line up other rooms for us in advance . . . Mike bristled!

Quotations from Night Clerk Mike:

"I have nothing to apologize to you for."

—2:10 A.M., November 15, 2001

Explaining why we were wrong to be upset that our "guaranteed" rooms weren't saved for us

The Career Path of Night Clerk Mike:

(He peaked last week.)

Mike Wasn't Too Optimistic About Finding Us a Place to Sleep.

2:15 in the morning is a heck of a time to start looking for two spare hotel rooms!

Mike slowly started dialing around town.

Quotations from Night Clerk Mike:

"I don't know if there *are* any hotel rooms around here. . . . All these hotels are full."

—2:12 A.M., November 15, 2001

Just starting to look for alternate accommodation for us, even though he'd filled his own house up by 11:00 P.M.

Mike Finally Found Us Rooms Here.

Shoney's Inn & Suites is a dump.

It is six miles further away from downtown Houston, which makes a difference in morning rush-hour traffic.

Had we wanted to stay at Shoney's, we would have called them in the first place.

We could only get smoking rooms.

The Experience Mike Provided Deviated from Usual Treatment of an HHonors Gold Member.

We Are Very Unlikely to Return to the DoubleTree Club Houston.

Lifetime chances of dying in a bathtub: 1 in 10,455
(National Safety Council)

Chance of Earth being ejected from the solar system by the gravitational pull of a passing star: 1 in 2,200,000
(University of Michigan)

Chance of winning the U.K. Lottery: 1 in 13,983,816
(U.K. Lottery)

Chance of us returning to the DoubleTree Club Houston: worse than any of those

Good luck!

And give our best to Mike!

Farmer had no idea of the impact his e-mail presentation was about to have. His colleague's mother-in-law thought the e-mail was so funny that she sent it to a friend, who sent it a friend, and so on and so on . . .

Within a week, the e-mail had spread beyond anyone's control. Farmer got calls from all over the United States, as well as the world. And he was buried in e-mails—more than two hundred a day, many of them from people in the hotel business. One e-mail informed him that his presentation was now part of the curriculum at the Kellogg School of Business Management.

Hotel managers from as far away as Saigon, Abu Dhabi, and Senegal—even someone living in a yurt—wrote to congratulate him. Farmer's e-mail is testament to the price that a business can be made to pay when one seemingly insignificant customer service disaster resonates disproportionately.

It wasn't long before Farmer heard from Hilton, the parent corporation of the DoubleTree brand. They first sent him room certificates for free hotel stays, but he sent them back. They asked for a meeting, following which Farmer told them he'd be happy if Hilton donated to his favorite charity, Toys for Tots. They did.

As things happened, this was not just some obscure footnote in Internet history. "Beyond that," says Farmer, "it turns out my little e-mail became a huge wake-up call for customer service training."

Interestingly enough, Mike the night clerk soon became a sort of cult figure. So many people were showing up at the hotel asking for him that they took him off the front desk for "retraining." But it was too late. Hilton dropped this particular DoubleTree from its portfolio, and the hotel became a Ramada Inn.

And what happened to night clerk Mike? Let's just say that no one knows and no one cares.

There's a somewhat happy ending to this story. Farmer says he is now on friendly terms with corporate management at DoubleTree. They even use his PowerPoint presentation as an internal training tool for frontline hotel workers.

Despite his shabby treatment at the DoubleTree, Tom Farmer learned the hard but valuable lesson that having a guaranteed room reservation held on a credit card does *not* necessarily mean the hotel is holding a room for you. It guarantees only that the hotel will be paid if you don't show up. In the Double-Tree case, the hotel was rolling the dice and accepting walk-ins, betting that Farmer wouldn't show up and it could pocket that money as well.

You can't afford to gamble. It's still a good idea to hold the room with a credit card, but the real responsibility here—at least in terms of guaranteeing that your room will be available when you arrive—rests with you.

Call the hotel and confirm the reservation on the day before you start traveling. Be sure to make note of the name and position of the person you speak with. Then, on the day you leave, call back and update the hotel on your arrival time, especially if you anticipate being late (or if you expect to arrive early). This tactic helps to ensure that the hotel will have your room ready by the time you get there, especially if there is a heavy checkout load just before your arrival. Your call alerts the hotel to instruct the housekeeping staff to attend to your room first.

THE FINE ART OF COMPLAINING

In the service industry, it's not the delivery of the service that ultimately makes the difference between a good, bad, or extraordinary experience. It's the *recovery*.

And in the hotel business, there are some legendary examples of recovery. In almost every case, the recovery not only saved the day but was the strongest motivation for the guest to return.

Consider the example of the doorman at the Four Seasons Hotel in the Georgetown section of Washington, D.C.

One early morning, two guests were checking out of the hotel at about the same time. The first, a businessman, was heading to Dulles Airport for a nonstop return flight to San Francisco. The second guest, an advertising executive, was getting a taxi for Reagan National Airport for the shuttle flight to LaGuardia in New York, where she was scheduled to make a crucial presentation to a key client later that day.

Somehow, the bellstaff mixed the bags at the hotel; the businessman's bags were put in the advertising executive's taxi, and vice versa. About twenty minutes later, the hotel received a panicked call from the advertising executive. She had arrived at National and discovered she had the wrong bags. To make matters worse, her luggage, containing all the materials essential for her presentation, was headed for Dulles with someone she didn't know—and her big moment in New York was only four hours away.

The doorman swung into action. Working with the concierge, he had the hotel call the airline at Dulles to intercept the businessman at the counter, where the woman's bags would be held. In the meantime, the doorman hopped into a taxi and raced to Dulles. On the way, he phoned the advertising executive and asked her what time her presentation was and the location of the meeting. He told her to check in the businessman's bags and take them with her to New York.

Upon arrival in Dulles, the doorman retrieved the woman's bags, jumped on a commuter flight to New York, and raced into the city, where he caught up with the advertising executive in time for her to make her do-or-die presentation. He also retrieved the executive's bags and FedExed them to San Francisco.

Now, *that's* recovery. But what is even more important about this story is that the doorman didn't ask permission to do any of this. He didn't fill out any forms or wait for any bureaucratic decisions. He just did it on his own initiative.

And what did this cost the hotel? When all was said and done, about $800 in airfares, taxis, and FedEx charges. But what was it worth? Both guests were so impressed by what the doorman had done that they now stay only at the Four Seasons.

Most of the time, however, the recovery happens after the fact. When a recovery is late or is forced by third parties, then the damage has already been done.

I remember my first visit to the Ilikai in Honolulu many years ago. An older hotel, it still had some attractive qualities. It's far enough removed from the noise of the hordes of tourists on Kalakaua Avenue, and it's at least ten minutes closer to the airport. The views are excellent and—another plus—rooms at the Ilikai come with fully equipped kitchens.

But my three-day stay there provided an interesting—and disappointing—glimpse at what can happen when an older hotel loses its touch, when a number of ownership and management changes combine to turn a once well-run hotel into nothing more than a high-rise collection of aging rooms.

First, some history. The Ilikai was built in 1964, as a luxurious 681-room addition to Waikiki Beach. It was later expanded to 800 rooms.

For almost twenty years, the hotel was managed by Westin and was known as the Westin Ilikai. Then, faced with the prospect of investing millions of dollars to renovate the hotel, Westin decided to explore the alternative of selling it. But there were few takers.

In 1983, Westin tried another idea: marketing one wing of the hotel as luxury time-share condominiums. But Westin spent little money in refurbishing the rooms or the hotel's public areas, and the condominiums flopped. Other deals fell through, and the hotel was sold to a private investment company and management firm. And then it was sold again.

Had enough history? Here's the story. By the time I got there, it was clear that little had been done to upgrade and improve the hotel. The lobby looked exactly as it had looked when the hotel originally opened for business. The metallic Westin logo had been removed from the wooden wall behind the front desk, but nothing replaced it—its outline could still be clearly seen, a ghostly reminder of a better past.

I had to wait ten minutes to check in. There were three cashiers on duty, doing nothing, but no one volunteered to handle incoming guests.

When it was my turn, I approached the counter, credit card in hand, ready to be imprinted. The clerk verified my reservation, but didn't want to take my credit card.

"I need to see two pieces of identification," she said, "both with photos."

I was late for an appointment, my wallet was locked in my bag, and I was confused by the request. "Why do you need that?" I asked.

"It's just our procedure," she replied.

This was the first time I had heard such a request at a hotel anyplace other than in a country involved in a major civil war. "Look," I tried to explain, "I'm very late, my wallet is locked away, and I don't really think this is necessary, since I've already been preregistered."

"But I need to see the IDs," she insisted.

I couldn't believe this. I pulled out my airline ticket. "See this?" I asked. "The ticket says 'Greenberg.' See my credit card? It says 'Greenberg.' See my bags? The tags say 'Greenberg.' Now unless there's some guy named Greenberg lying facedown at the airport, you're just going to have to take my word that I'm Greenberg. In the meantime, I'll be glad to give you my credit card so you can take an imprint."

"No," she insisted. "I don't need your credit card. I need *two* IDs."

"Well," I said, taking the room key, "it will just have to wait." And I headed for my room.

I ducked into the bathroom to take a quick shower before dinner, but there was neither soap nor towels. I picked up the phone to call housekeeping, but the connection was so bad that they couldn't hear me. I called back and yelled my room number into the phone along with the words "towels," "soap," and hung up.

I quickly scanned the room. The view, as expected, was terrific. But where were the smoke detectors? The sprinklers? None were apparent. I did not find this reassuring, especially when I realized I was staying on the twenty-fifth floor.

It was after midnight when I returned from dinner. The towels—one stained with what appeared to be cigarette burns—had indeed arrived, along with the soap. I got undressed and took my long-awaited shower, then went to bed.

At 2 A.M., the phone on the desk suddenly rang. In the darkness, I felt my way across the room to answer it. I managed to pick it up on the third ring, but all I got was a dial tone. As I put the receiver down, the red message light suddenly began flashing. I called downstairs. The phone rang twenty times (I counted) before someone answered, and the connection was horrendous.

"Excuse me," I said, "but my message light just went on."

There was a long pause while the operator checked. "Are you Mr. Donaldson?" she asked.

"No, I'm Mr. Greenberg."

"Greenberg?"

"Yes."

"I have one message for you. Please come down to the front desk with two pieces of identification."

I hung up and tried to go back to sleep.

At 7:45 the next morning, the maid came barging into my room, without knocking. I yelled, and she left. Then the phone rang again. I raced to answer it. Again, I was greeted by a dial tone. This time I hung up the receiver and just stared at the message light. Sure enough, it flashed. Again, I dialed the message desk. No, I was not Mr. Donaldson. And the message? You guessed it: "Please come down to the front desk with two pieces of identification."

"But I'm not Mr. Donaldson!" I again objected.

Still the clerk stubbornly insisted that this was the policy of the hotel.

"Look, until you can explain this policy to me, I won't do it," I said. And I hung up the phone. If I were paranoid, I might be inclined to think the hotel was out to get me. In fact, during the next day and a half, I received three more similar messages and no explanations of the policy.

Then the phone system broke down entirely, and important business messages were coming in four hours late. The final blow was the hotel newsstand incident. On my last morning, I entered the lobby newsstand to purchase a Sunday paper, some magazines, and some diet sodas. The tab was $12.75. I showed the clerk my key and asked to charge it to my room. No, she didn't ask to see two pieces of ID. Instead, she called the front desk for authorization. After ten long minutes (with an angry line of customers waiting behind me), she got through.

"I'm sorry, sir," she said. "Your charge has been denied. It seems they don't have your credit card imprint."

My credit card imprint? That's what I offered them when I checked in, which the front desk clerk refused. That did it. Angrily, I marched to the front desk. I demanded to see the manager. He wasn't around. I demanded to see *any* hotel management official. None could be found. The woman at the front desk assured me that someone would "get in touch."

Forty minutes later, after a newspaperless breakfast, I returned to my room. I was greeted—again—with the red flashing message light. Surely, I surmised, this must be the manager trying to get in touch with me.

I called downstairs.

"Mr. Donaldson?" the clerk asked again.

"No," I answered sarcastically, "I'm his new best friend, Mr. Greenberg."

There was a pause. "Oh, yes, Mr. Greenberg. The message is 'Can you please come downstairs with two pieces of ID?' "

There was nothing for me to do but laugh—and then quickly

check out. And, of course, I never heard anything from the management of the hotel.

In subsequent years, this hotel has been renovated a number of times. But one issue persists: a facelift means nothing if the personality of the hotel remains a major problem.

So how do you fight back?

At the *Today* show, we put together a series each year called "Getaways Gone Wrong." And each year, the horror stories concerning hotels seem to get worse. Hotels and resorts watch this series with a combination of fear and readiness—fear of having a disaster story about them told on national television, and readiness to launch into major recovery mode. Our researchers check each story thoroughly to verify the details, as well as the chronology of the tales of travel woe. But once these episodes are broadcast, it's amazing for us to watch how quickly those mentioned in the segments rush to make restitution for their transgressions and offer to give full refunds.

Tom Farmer used his PowerPoint presentation to fight back. I am lucky enough to have the forum of national television. Although you might not have such a public platform, you still have the power to call attention to problems that need redress. Your strength in launching an effective complaint is in attention to the details.

If you have the skills of a good reporter, half the complaint battle is won. The sheer merit of your case is not necessarily enough to enable you to win. You need to uncover those details, including full names and dates.

The real bottom line in the art of complaining is that you need to do some homework first. Establish a record of what exactly happened. Get first and last names, as well as titles, of the people involved in the situation. Many frequent travelers of normal intelligence fail to do this before attempting to make their case.

Here are some tips to help you document and get results from your complaints:

- Create a paper trail.

- Alexander Anolik, a San Francisco–based attorney who specializes in travel law (see Chapter 11), recommends carrying a $6 throwaway camera on all your trips—not just to record the great vacation memories, but to visually document any complaints that might arise.

- Never take no as an answer from someone who is not empowered to say yes to you in the first place.

CHAPTER 5

What the Bellhop and Doorman Won't Tell You

CHECKING IN

If you think about it, the bellhops actually are the ones who know which rooms are the best at any hotel. After all, they've been inside every single one of them.

So when a bellhop takes you to your room, you have nothing to lose by asking him (or her) if *he* actually likes the room you've been given. You'd be taken aback at how often he doesn't. However, if tipped properly, he can sometimes arrange to change that room through one of his friends at the front desk.

Even if the hotel is officially overbooked, the bellhop also knows the unadvertised rooms that might be available. (And by now, so should you.)

In an oversell situation, ask the bellhop to show you one of these:

- *A suite connector room.* Often a hotel doesn't sell the entire suite, which leaves the sitting room portion, usually connected to the suite by a lockable door, available. If the sofa in that room doesn't convert to a bed, the hotel can bring a bed in. The bottom line is that the room rate will be discounted accordingly.

- *An "out-of-order" room.* It's highly unusual that all the available rooms at a hotel are deemed ready for occupancy. An out-of-order room might have a stain on the carpet or a defective television—something that would take it out of the main room inventory. Therefore, an overbooked hotel might not really be considered sold out if you factor in the out-of-order rooms. In such situations, some managers might just release one of these rooms to you at a distressed, discount, last-sell price.

When Is a Guest Not a Guest?

If you're checking into a hotel and your room isn't ready, your bags may simply be left on a luggage cart in the lobby. You must insist that they be put away in a holding or storage room, properly identified, with individual numbered hotel luggage tags on each bag.

Even so, you are not legally protected from loss. If your bags contain any valuables, you need to ask that the bags be put in the hotel safe, even if you haven't officially checked in. At the very least, request that the valuable contents of those bags be placed inside one of the hotel's safe-deposit boxes.

Merely leaving bags with the bellhop is a prescription for trouble. Although it may be convenient, you may not have any legal rights if those bags disappear. Bellhops get busy, and in busy hotel lobbies it's easy for bags to vanish.

Consider the case of Salisbury versus the St. Regis–Sheraton Hotel Corporation, which dates back to 1978, although the principles still apply today. On November 22, 1978, Mr. and Mrs. Roger Salisbury finished a three-day stay at the St. Regis Sheraton in New York. (The St. Regis is now simply called the St. Regis but, like Sheraton, is now part of Starwood Hotels.) While Mr. Salisbury checked out, returned his room key, and paid the bill, Mrs. Salisbury checked all their luggage with a bellhop in the lobby. The Salisburys planned to return to the hotel later in the day and retrieve their bags.

When the couple returned at 4:30 that afternoon, one of the bags, a cosmetics case containing jewelry worth more than $60,000, was missing. The Salisburys sued the hotel.

The hotel argued that Mrs. Salisbury did not inform the hotel of the value of the cosmetics bag and she did not ask that the case be kept in the hotel's safe, nor did she inform the hotel that the contents of the bag exceeded $100. Indeed, the hotel seemed to be protected based on Sections 200 and 201 of the New York General Business Law, which set limits on the liability of hoteliers and innkeepers as long as they provide safes. Thus, citing these provisions, the hotel moved for the case to be dismissed.

However, the Salisbury attorneys counterclaimed that these rules applied only to hotel guests, and since the Salisburys had checked out before the incident occurred, they were no longer deemed guests. This raised a critical question that seems to crop up in many travel law cases: at what point does someone cease to be considered a guest?

In this particular case, the court relied on two other cases— one dating back to 1940 and the other to 1911. In the 1940 case, a guest stored his steamer trunks at a hotel. When he came back to claim them seven years later, they were gone. The hotel had sold them. When he sued, the court ruled that the relationship in question was not that of an innkeeper and a guest but, rather, that of a bailee and bailor. He received no compensation.

In the second case, a hotel guest had left his horse at an inn while he continued his journey by train. During his absence, something happened to the horse. Again, the court ruled that he was not a hotel guest. Compensation? Nada.

In the Salisbury case, the court stated that the luggage had not been left for seven years but for less than seven hours, and the hotel had accepted that luggage as an accommodation to the couple. The case was dismissed. The Salisburys received nothing.

The moral of this story is that if you have valuables and want the hotel to store them, regardless of whether you are a current or recently departed guest, leaving them with the bellhop doesn't protect you in any way.

Making a Dead Move

If you arrive at a hotel and your room isn't ready, you certainly have the option to ask whether the hotel has another room you can use to shower and change in until your own room is available. Many hotels will allow for this. However, an important word of caution: when your hotel room does finally become available, you may not be around. In that case, the hotel will sometimes—with your permission, but often without it—perform "dead move." This means that the staff will go to the room you are temporarily using—without you in it—pack up your stuff and move it to the original room you reserved.

There are problems inherent in dead moves. First, you might presume that the hotel staff will not pack your belongings without thoroughly sweeping the room for things you may have left inside. That presumption would be incorrect.

Second, the highest incidence of "unexplained disappearances" of guest property at hotels occurs during dead moves. If you're not in the room when the move is performed, your legal standing is diminished. It's your word versus theirs, and rarely can you recover the loss. Therefore, it is important to insist that the hotel not be permitted to move your belongings unless you are present for the move.

To Schlep or Not to Schlep

And now a word about your stuff *before* it gets to the hotel. Are you still schlepping it, or have you figured a way to minimize that burden en route? The answer, at least for me, is to embrace the notion that there are two kinds of airline bags: carry-on and lost. So I don't check bags. I FedEx them. (You can also use UPS, DHL, or any other courier service.)

You might be afraid that the cost would be a deterrent. It's not how much it costs, however, but how much it's *worth* in terms of your time. Every time I fly domestically, I save an average of two hours of my life by not checking bags. By using a courier to deliver my bags to my destination, I avoid the need to haul them to the airport and wait in a long line to have them inspected. When I land, I don't have to stand around with the other schleppers at the baggage carousel, hoping against hope that my bags might have been on the same flight I was. And if I get lucky and they *were* on the flight, in the time it takes me to retrieve the bags I have been caught in another long line for a taxi, which in turn will likely get caught in rush-hour traffic.

I FedEx the bags directly to my hotel. And there's a method to that madness: since I usually know where I'm going at least a day or two ahead of time, I don't have to rush-ship them via FedEx. I check the box on the packing slip that sends the bags on a two- or three-day advance trip for a discount. Then I call the hotel and speak to the bellstaff, giving them the tracking number from the FedEx waybill. Since I'm also preregistered for my room, I can ask the bellstaff to deliver my bags to my room before I even arrive. How great is that?

Be aware, however, that if you don't call ahead and talk to the bellstaff, your bags may end up in the hotel's receiving department, and no one at the front desk will even know they are there. So always call ahead.

CELEBRITY BELLHOP: Tom Hanks once worked as a bellhop at the Oakland, California, Hilton. He didn't particularly like the job, but every once in a while he got a chance to drive celebrities to and from the airport. His most memorable ride was driving Bill Cosby—memorable, according to Hanks, because Cosby didn't tip him.

My experience is that once the bellstaff is on top of a situation, they stay on top if it. There is a very good reason for this: bellhops see everything. They know every nook and cranny of their hotel. They know who is sleeping with whom and, for that matter, who isn't sleeping with whom. And they're usually wired into everything local.

I've found that while the concierge at a hotel can charter a fishing boat, the bellhop can actually take you fishing. If you're staying at a hotel for more than a night or planning a return to that hotel, it's a good idea (and sometimes a spectacular one) to establish a relationship with the bellhop.

More than just giving you a guided tour to your room when you check in (after all, how difficult is it to find the ice machine?), the bellhop is the navigator on your starship *Enterprise*.

CHECKING OUT

Whenever I'm checking out, I ask for the bellhop about five minutes before I plan to actually vacate the room. Once I'm convinced I've finished packing, I enlist the help of the bellhop, and together we make a sweep of the room in a clockwise manner from entry to entry to ensure that nothing ends up in lost-and-found hell. Then, and only then, do I leave the room and check out.

The last thing you want is for your bags to go down to the lobby and just sit there unattended. If a friend is picking you up, describe the type of car your friend is driving and ask the bellhop to load the car. If you're going to hail a cab, ask the bellhop to do that and load your bags into the cab as well.

The Role of the Doorman

This brings us to the subject of one of the most powerful people in the hotel—the doorman (yes, there are doorwomen, but very few).

> Doorman—a genius who can open the door of your car with one hand, help you with the other, and still have one left for the tip.
>
> —*Dorothy Kilgallen*

Many hotel guests view the doorman—presuming the hotel has one—as a gratuitous convenience who opens doors, hails cabs, and assists with luggage. But a doorman is much more than that. He basically runs the joint—or at least the outside real estate that surrounds it. He controls traffic, both human and motorized, in and out of the hotel. He determines who parks what, and where, and for how long. In many cases, he is the Godfather of taxis, arbitrating which companies get the best fares. At many hotels, the doorman acts as the unofficial lookout for regular guests who need to be alerted if a wife or husband makes a sudden, unexpected, and unwelcome visit. He may also be responsible—unofficially, of course—for escorting certain other unannounced guests into and out of the hotel, with the operative goal being to preserve their status as anonymous and also, hopefully, unwitnessed.

Second only to the concierge (see Chapter 8), the doorman is a very powerful person at a hotel. In fact, at most major city hotels, after the general manager, it's the doorman who makes the most money. I am not exaggerating when I tell you that at some New York hotels, when the doorman finally retires, he sells his position! It's worth that much.

How much exactly? Let's do the math. At a busy hotel in a city like New York, Chicago, or Boston, the doorman hails cabs for guests, most of whom tip $1, and he unloads luggage from incoming guest cars and taxis, which usually merits another $1 tip per bag.

I followed one Chicago doorman throughout his shift. During that time, he never sat down (except to move a car), never ate, drank, or even left for a bathroom break. And with good reason: the money.

When he finished his shift, I followed him to an employee break area and asked him to empty his pockets so we could count the tip money. In one eight-hour shift, his tip money came to $478! Furthermore, he told me that it had been a slow night, that he often can bring in $600 a night. But even if a doorman averages $400 a night, five nights a week, that's an unreported income of more than $100,000 a year, not counting the doorman's base salary.

In many cases, a doorman's income is even more than that because of the relationship he has with taxi and limo drivers. The first thing cab drivers do is make friends with the doorman, with an obvious motive: preferred position. The cab drivers want the airport runs rather than the short hops, and the doorman is the designated taxi traffic controller.

When you exit a big city hotel, you may notice a small line of waiting taxis. However, you don't hail the cab—the doorman does, and then only after asking you where you want to go. The doorman selects the particular cab that will take you there.

In New York, this business is conducted by using finger signals. A raised index finger means a trip to Kennedy Airport, two fingers means LaGuardia, and three fingers means Newark. The fingers also signify something else: the kickback the doorman often receives for distributing the best fares. If you tell the doorman you're only going ten blocks, he won't signal the waiting taxi line—he'll walk a few feet in front of the hotel and hail a cruising cab.

The doorman also controls which limousines can park in front of the hotel, as well as whether your car gets parked in the darkest depths of the hotel garage or at the curb in front of the hotel's main entrance. It all comes down to money. If the hotel charges, say, $37 a night for parking (many big city hotels charge at least that much), parking charges could easily add another 25 percent to your total hotel bill. But if you tip the doorman $20 to park the car in front rather than in the garage, it's a win-win situation for both of you. Trust me, it's what he wants you to do. Many hotels, as well as many doormen, practice a form of blatant extortion when it comes to ground transporation and who gets to do business in front of the hotel.

The Los Angeles *Daily News* followed the paper trail of an actual bidding war among doormen and local cab companies for the exclusive right to pick up hotel guests from particular hotels. L.A.'s Checker cab cooperative was paying $500,000 a year to different hotels. The Century Plaza gets $20,000 a month just from one taxi company that wants the exclusive right to pick up guests. The same company was paying the Hyatt Regency $140,000 a year for the same right.

Like many other cities, Los Angeles operates by kickbacks. And frequently the money gets funneled from limousine and taxi companies directly through—or to—hotel doormen. So the next time you get a chance to speak to a hotel doorman, ask him how he likes his summer place in the Hamptons or the weekend beach house he owns in Malibu. Then, while he's trying to figure out how you know about that, ask him to hail you a cab.

TIPPING GUIDE

What would be an appropriate tip these days when you check into your hotel?

First of all, heavy lifting should always be rewarded. If someone takes your overstuffed suitcase out of your trunk or brings it up to your room, figure on tipping at least $1 a bag, and twice that in big cities. However, if an assistant manager shows you to your room, don't tip. He or she is a part of management and, in fact, should refuse money if you offer it.

What about room service? (See also Chapter 10.) Most hotels add a service charge to the bill. Some guests don't notice that, and, I imagine, many a room service waiter has skipped back down the hall with a 30 percent tip. It's acceptable to simply ask, "Is service included in the bill?" That way, servers know you mean to acknowledge their efforts. If someone has gone beyond the call of duty or if the built-in gratuity is only 10 or 12 percent, you might want to add a few bucks on top.

Better hotels offer a concierge desk to help you with restaurant or theater reservations. Any extraordinary effort by a concierge, such as securing sold-out tickets, deserves a ten- or twenty-spot. Much of the concierge's income comes from tips. At one hotel where I stay regularly, I have a unique and mutually satisfactory arrangement with the concierge: I tip him, once each year, by cashing in my airline mileage and giving him a flight anywhere he wants to go in the United States.

Americans still aren't accustomed to tipping housekeepers, who may have the most thankless jobs in any hotel. Leave a few bucks for every day that you stay. Better yet, tip your housekeeper in person when you *arrive*—that way you know the right person is getting the cash, and you might find an extra mint on your pillow or a bottle of shower gel in your bathroom.

Not every hotel you stay in will have a bellhop and concierge on staff. More often than not, hotels have Joe, or Billy, or Frank, who is a minimum-wage employee asleep behind the desk when you arrive. In such cases, you needn't worry because tipping is probably not expected. But if you're staying in a place that is slightly more upscale, tipping is both customary and appreciated.

Because tipping is a way of rewarding good service, there is no way to say what is appropriate across the board. Tip at your own discretion and only if you feel it is warranted. Here are some guidelines to follow:

- *Valet:* $1 to $2 each time the valet gets your car, and more in bad weather.

- *Shuttle driver:* $2.

- *Doorman:* $1 to $2 for hailing a cab.

- *Bellhop:* $1 to $2 a bag if he brings your bags up to your room and again when he carries them down.

- *Concierge:* The concierge at a hotel is your main man or woman. If you need any kind of arrangements made during your stay, he or she can often make you dinner reservations, get you theater tickets, and in general attend to you for anything you need. It is a good idea to tip the concierge the first time you request special attention—anywhere from $2 to $20, depending on the service provided and the services you anticipate needing. (See also Chapter 8.)

WHO MAKES WHAT: The travel industry accounts for 6 percent of the entire U.S. workforce. Salaries for hotel employees range widely. A general manager with a few years on the job in a posh midtown Manhattan hotel could easily pull down six figures a year, according to the American Hotel and Lodging Association (AHLA).

SALARIES:

• **General manager** at properties with over 200 rooms:	$90,000
• **General manager** at properties with fewer than 90 rooms:	$35,000
Median salary for all GMs in 2002:	$55,620
• **Executive chef**	$51,500
• **Director of food and beverage**	$48,925
• **Rooms manager**	$46,350
• **Restaurant manager**	$32,960
• **Executive housekeeper**	$30,274
• **Bell captain**	$17,065
• **Bell staff**	$14,420
• **Doorman** anywhere from $20,000 to $100,000	

- *Room service:* 15 percent of the bill, or at least $2, unless gratuity is included.

- *Housekeeping:* $1 to $5 per night, depending on how neat you are.

- *Coat check:* $1 to $2.

CHAPTER 6

The People Who Design Hotel Rooms Have Never Stayed in One

The bedrooms are just large enough for a well-
behaved dwarf and a greyhound on a diet.

—*John Russell*

"We have a lovely room for you," says the front desk clerk, as you check into your hotel. Indeed, when the bellhop takes you to your room, it does look lovely. He points out the ice bucket and the thermostat, he opens the curtains, and he shows you the television. Everything looks to be in place.

But that's the problem—it's not *your* place, and you quickly discover that nothing works the way it's supposed to work. The curtains don't open all the way. The bathroom is lit too dimly, and you constantly run into the armoire on your way to the toilet. The remote control to the television is bolted to the nightstand. And, oh yes, you can't see the television from the nonfunctional minidesk, and you get a stiff neck trying to watch it from your bed. The closet is too narrow to hang your garment bag inside and still close the door. And the phone is attached to a cord that is only two feet from the wall—it is virtually unmovable.

BACK IN THE U.S.S.R.: Tacked on the door of a Moscow hotel room during the Soviet era: "If this is your first visit to the U.S.S.R., you are welcome to it."

Welcome to the continuing nightmare of poor hotel room design. In many hotels, it seems like the furniture, the equipment, and even the plumbing are designed more for the convenience of the hotel than for that of the guest.

Hoteliers are not designers. And those who own hotels need a return on their investment. Result: badly designed hotels.

The first problem a guest encounters often has to do with room lighting and, specifically, one of my pet peeves—the master switch. Ever notice that hotels put the master switch near the front door? Guests entering the room push the switch, and all the room lights go on. But there is one small problem: there is no master switch by the bed. At night when guests want to go to bed, they have to go to the door, hit the switch, and then stumble back to the bed without injuring themselves. The bedside table lamps do a great job of lighting up the bedside table, but nothing else—including what you are trying to read.

And then there's the furniture itself. When hotel operators don't think things through thoroughly, they buy room furniture in bits and pieces. As a result, I've been in more than a few hotels where the beds sit higher than the television cabinet—you can see the screen only if you're sitting on the end of the bed or lying on the floor.

STYLE OVER SUBSTANCE

> It used to be a good hotel, but that proves nothing.
> I used to be a good boy . . .
> —*Mark Twain*

Just because a hotel has been newly renovated does not guarantee that the owners or managers have been able to remedy basic design flaws. An existing structure does not always allow for sweeping changes. In older buildings, designers can't really move plumbing, so they concentrate on such things as lighting and full-length mirrors.

However, there are few excuses for bad design in new hotel construction. I remember when Marriott opened a new hotel in Hong Kong. The management prided itself on state-of-the-art room design—or so they said.

Everything in the guest rooms could be controlled by a bedside panel—the lights, the television, even the curtains were operated electronically from the panel. When guests opened closets, lights miraculously turned on. However, the electric curtains did not open the full width of the windows. Within a few days, many of them were broken as guests manually pulled, then yanked, them open.

HIGH CONCEPT IN GERMANY: If you're tired of the bland anonymity of hotel rooms with muted colors, Gideon Bibles, and subpar pay-per-view options, hop a plane to Berlin and book a room at the Propeller Island City Lodge. Created by German artist and musician Lars Stroschen, each of the hotel's thirty rooms features its own freakish high-concept theme. Kick back in the Upside Down Room, complete with prison bars, a cot, and an escape tunnel, or reflect a while in the Mirror Room, paneled entirely in mirrors. Overly enthusiastic guests sometimes come dressed in outfits to match their theme rooms. Still not German enough for you? Stroschen has also composed a different soothing techno soundtrack for each room. Although the hotel is hugely popular with curious travelers, Stroschen had a lot of trouble convincing city officials that the $1.5 million project wouldn't become a logistical nightmare.

In a Hilton Garden Inn out near the airport in El Segundo in Los Angeles, you'll find a one-of-a-kind concept room. Hilton calls it "the Room of the Future." Not just a display room, the Room of the Future has been fully operational since the hotel opened in 2000. What's amazing about the room is that it is standard in size—about three hundred square feet—and yet the designers have thought of just about everything within that footprint.

They've created extra space by angling the bed and the furniture. They've also improved the lighting and made the entire room user-friendly. Then there's the technology, starting with a forty-two-inch flat-screen plasma TV with full in-room entertainment features, including a DVD/CD player and a receiver with surround sound speakers. But that's just the beginning. The room also offers these features:

- Flat-screen LCD monitor installed next to the bathtub

- Touch panel that controls the entertainment functions, lighting, and drapes

- High-speed Internet access over the television or the laptop computer

- Ergonomic chair and workspace

- Fully articulating king-size "sleep system," featuring a system of air baffles and slats instead of typical coil springs, that automatically adjust to the contours of the guest's body

- Automated climate control system that turns on when the guest enters

- Motion-sensitive entryway lights that illuminate when the guest enters

- Smart-card lock system, allowing guests to use a personal smart card, such as their own credit card, to access the room without needing an additional room key

- Biometric safe, which is locked and unlocked using only the guest's fingerprint

- Cordless phone

- Leather massage lounge chair

- Ionic air purifier

- Electronic "Do Not Disturb/Make Up Room" sign

- Jacuzzi tub and modern bathroom design

- Automatic defogging mirror

- Integrated toilet/bidet with heated seat

- Shower with five automated jets

- Electric towel warmer

- Mini-refrigerator featuring electronic compressorless technology

- Built-in ironing board with cordless iron

- Oxygen ionizer

But the wildest innovation in this room is the self-sanitizing bathroom.

At the Embassy Suites Hotel in New York, another room experiment caught my eye. It is called the "Creativity Suite," a two room eye-grabber complete with floor-to-ceiling chalkboard, seating cushions on the floor, and even a shower with a wall suitable for writing notes during creative bathroom thinking time—another room of the future.

I must admit that I really liked these rooms of the future. But wait a minute—if these rooms are so cool, if everything in them works, and if the design and technology are available today, why aren't they the rooms of the *present?*

The answer is simple: money. Few hotels want to invest the money needed to ensure common sense, functionality, and guest comfort in their room designs. And so, except for that place in El Segundo, we're left with the less-than-satisfactory rooms of the present.

It might surprise you to learn that 25 percent of travelers are responsible for one half of all U.S. hotel revenue. These are the repeat guests—myself among them—to whom design and functionality of hotel rooms makes the difference in whether or not we return to the same hotel.

Hotel designer Dan Nelson, who has designed everything from the Windsor Court in New Orleans to the newly opened Wyndham on the Puerto Rican island of Vieques, once told me that the problem with most hotels is that "they're really nothing more than hospitals with much nicer carpets." That's a distressing thought, but Nelson may have a point. The association with hospital design is unfortunate, but why should we be satisfied with it?

Some history is in order. Hotels were first designed for people of means and power, so designers used large quantities of gold leaf and ornamentation as representative of their status. Lobbies were grand statements. Bathrooms, however, were afterthoughts.

Then came the concept of hotels as glass monoliths, complete with large atria. Although they may have been architecturally spectacular, they did not make the guests who stayed there more comfortable.

About twenty years ago, the major international hotel chains decided they wanted more control over design, and they wanted to reclaim the space lost to some of the more elaborate design features—so good-bye, atria. However, this resulted in the so-

---

UNDERGROUND HOTEL: Many hotels have a special room set aside for unexpected V.I.P. guests. The posh Greenbrier Hotel (on U.S. 60, White Sulphur Springs, West Virginia) has eight hundred such rooms. In the late 1950s, the government built a cavernous fallout shelter beneath the resort. It includes separate subterranean meeting chambers for the Senate and House of Representatives. The *Washington Post* blew the Greenbrier site's cover in 1992 and since then, the government isn't sure it wants to maintain the facility. The Greenbrier is merely the toniest of a whole string of federal fallout shelters in the mountains west of Washington. Unusual for a bomb shelter, the Greenbrier facility is leased. The reported rent ($50,000 to $60,000 a year) isn't so bad considering that you'd need about $35 million to rent all seven hundred of the Greenbrier's aboveground units for a year.

---

called cookie-cutter rooms, which were mostly interchangeable, and bathroom design was again an afterthought. Competitive hotel frequent-stay programs kept customers loyal in order to earn points, but they didn't keep them happy. Most hotel rooms of this period were dimly lit and barely functional. Desks didn't hold anything more than a parade of promotional tent cards. We stayed in these hotel rooms because we were held captive by those loyalty programs.

Designer hotels were the next phase. The lobbies continued to make a statement. The public rooms—dining rooms and bars—attracted a lot of media buzz. But the guest rooms? Guess what—we still hated them.

There are designer hotels and then there are hotels that are designed well, with rooms and features that actually function. Many of my friends are in denial when it comes to designer hotels. In the typical style-over-substance dilemma, they mistakenly choose style. They find themselves walking into a poorly designed, dimly lit lobby, where the staff looks like they've all escaped from an old Robert Palmer video. They are taken to their rooms—small, minimalist cubicles that are nothing less than obstacle courses of eye-catching but potentially hazardous furniture. Their bathrooms have bad, dim mood lighting (translation: within fifteen seconds of entering the bathroom, you're in a bad mood), and even though there's a very cool-looking stainless steel sink in the center, there is literally no shelf space on which to put any of their stuff.

WATER WORLD: Guests can swim a mile and still not get to the end of the pools and waterways at the Melia Cancun Resort. The five pools and waterways gracefully curve around three sides of the hotel, so that pool guests can follow the sun from dawn to sunset.

Then there's the truly dysfunctional part. For the next two or three days, they reside in denial. It's supposed to be a cool hotel, and they tell everyone they're staying in a cool hotel, and part of them really wants to believe it's a cool hotel. But the reality is that (with all due apologies to the legendary vaudeville comedian Henny Youngman) the rooms are so small that guests have to leave their rooms to change their minds.

I remember checking into the W Hotel on 49th Street and Lexington in Manhattan. It was (and still is) billed as a designer hotel, with a slick approach to hospitality, whatever that means. The lobby wasn't just busy—it was downright crowded with the overflow from the trendy designer bar. I practically had to run a gauntlet of hipper-than-hip bar patrons to get to the front desk. I couldn't hear the stylishly dressed desk clerk because of the noise. I was then escorted to my "suite." When the bellhop opened the door, I thought I was looking at another corridor—but I was actually looking at the room, which could barely hold the bed. The color scheme was white on white (my interpretation of that: don't touch anything, don't sit anywhere). The bathroom was so small that it was virtually impossible to be inside it and close the door without hitting (or perhaps even hurting) yourself. The decor was, naturally, minimalist, with a *Psycho III* shower curtain and no place to put any of my bathroom essentials. And that was considered a *suite!*

The one redeeming fixture in the room was the bed, which Westin had been marketing as a Heavenly Bed. Indeed it was, and the fit was so tight in the room that you couldn't really get out of bed on the side, but had to climb out at the foot of the bed.

Like many hotels of this type, the designers were confronted with an older building consisting of bedrooms with extremely small area and older bathrooms, with no opportunity to expand the square footage of either. So, with such limited space, they concentrated on the bed as their only hope. They found a manufacturer who developed a wide-width microdenier polyester fabric that gave the feel of combed cotton. Indeed, when people talk to me about that hotel, they always mention the bed—almost as if it had been the defining moment of their stay at the W. And, in fact, it probably was.

SIZE MATTERS

Many hotel interior designers face the same problem: they are confined by both budget and square footage. To compound matters, they tend to focus on the visual instead of the practical. They want rooms to look nice, and they try to do everything possible to disguise the smallness. They position extra mirrors in strategic places to give the impression that the room is larger than it actually is. They decorate with simple art reproductions because complicated artwork makes the room appear to shrink. That sounds like a fine approach. It might even look attractive. But does the room *work?* My room at the W certainly didn't.

HOW SMALL IS SMALL? The world's smallest full-service hotel rooms can be found at the 127-room WJ (also known as the Washington Jefferson). Measuring just seven by eleven feet, the room features just a twin bed, TV, and phone. That's it. Yes, the bed is tiny, but it does come with a goose-down comforter.

This situation can become an even bigger challenge for frequent travelers who come to embrace their hotel as their home. My friend Chris Woodyard, who writes for *USA Today*, reports that he spent forty-one days, one hour, and fifty-seven minutes living in the same hotel. This was not in Cleveland, mind you, but at the Marriott in Islamabad, Pakistan.

Not long after settling in, he tried to reorganize the room. He unplugged lamps, moved furniture around, rigged extension cords. He soon realized he couldn't make the room seem bigger or the bathroom seem any less spartan. Other than some books and a CD player he had brought with him, his room really was just like all the others. And so he decided to grin and bear it. He made that room his home for a little more than a month—and he lived to tell about the experience.

Woodyard wasn't in Pakistan by choice. But if he had had a choice, he would gladly—like most of us—have paid extra for the semblance of home, comfort, and functionality. Indeed, most guests are actually willing to pay significantly more per night for a higher level of comfort and more emotional satisfaction during their stay.

Many hotels exude elegance, but there's nothing warm about them. They also go to great lengths to promote their elegance, but elegance without warmth is arrogance.

Furthermore, size matters—but not necessarily in the ways you might think. It's not always how big the room is that makes the difference, but the proportions of the things that are in that room.

I once asked Bill Marriott when he had last stayed in just a regular room at one of his hotels. "Last night," he quickly replied. "I don't like suites," he continued. "Too many light switches to turn off."

There's another problem as well. The bigger the room, the more our amount of stuff seems to expand to fill it, and the more likely we are to lose things in that room.

WEAPONS OF MASS DISTRACTION

Remember, if it's not an option to increase the square footage of a room, the designers have to be that much more creative in delivering features that will elicit that satisfying emotional experience from hotel guests who stay in that room.

Not long ago, all hotel beds were low and flat—about twenty-one inches high, with seven-inch mattresses. Not anymore. An increasing number of hotels are now featuring eighteen-inch mattresses and beds that sit thirty-seven inches off the ground.

Then there's the bathroom, which is ground zero in my book for hotel design wars. We probably spend more waking hours in our hotel bathrooms than in any other room in the hotel. Lighting is key here, for both men and women, and shelf space is essential, especially for women. Anytime a hotel wants to spruce itself up, the designers install marble in the bathroom. But beware! It's a nice touch, but it can be hazardous because marble is so slippery when it's wet. Before entering a marble bath or shower, make sure you've located the grab rails or other hand-holds. When leaving a bath or shower in a heavily marbled bathroom, focus on your center of gravity. Lean forward, even if you are dripping wet, until you can make it to the carpeted bed-room, where you can safely dry yourself. Return to the bathroom only after you're dry.

Pedestal televisions are a nice idea that rarely live up to their potential because they are generally an afterthought. They are usually brought in after all the other furniture has been posi-tioned, and just because the television can swivel, that doesn't mean you can see it from any corner of the room. Typically, when you open the armoire containing the TV, the doors hit some other piece of furniture or swing back and obstruct the view.

I am inclined to measure a hotel's quality by the number of telephones in my room. When the Four Seasons opened its first hotel in Los Angeles in 1987, the place became an instant suc-cess. When I asked departing guests to describe why they liked the hotel so much, they were unable to. Was it the room size? No, the rooms were small. The health club? No, again too small. The pool? Also small. The ballroom? The hotel didn't have a ballroom. And yet people were raving about this hotel.

Finally, prompted by both frustration and curiosity, I checked into that hotel. Indeed, the rooms were small. But within five minutes I had figured out the hotel's edge in terms of design and function: the telephones.

There was a phone on each nightstand, one on the desk, one in the bathroom, and one near the balcony. Each phone had two lines, hold buttons, and call-waiting. The cords were extra long—if a fire broke out here, you could almost lower yourself out the balcony on the phone cord! The beauty of this hotel for business travelers is that they need never miss a call. They can work the room and do everything short of landing planes at the airport.

I had an amusing encounter shortly thereafter. Four Seasons was building its first resort hotel in Wailea, on the island of Maui. I visited the hotel during its construction and walked the grounds. Based on my phone experiences at the Four Seasons in Los Angeles, I asked the management how many phones they'd be putting in guest rooms.

"We did some focus group testing," the Four Seasons official responded, "and our customers told us they planned to be on vacation here, and didn't want to be disturbed. Therefore, we're only installing one small phone by the bed."

Mistake. I tried to explain that focus groups, for the most part, are in denial. They will tell companies either what they think the companies want to believe about them or, worse, what they would like to believe about themselves.

It wasn't at all that these people didn't want to be disturbed. They lived their lives as a never-ending series of disruptions. Although they wanted to think they'd be at the beach for eight hours with a piña colada in hand, the reality is that they would be on the beach for an hour, and then would want to log on to the Internet to find out the sports scores from the night before or to e-mail their friends to boast about how they were hanging loose in Maui.

The one-phone-per-room idea lasted barely two months. After an extensive (and expensive) rewiring, guests who check into the Four Seasons these days will find five phones in each room—four hardwired phones in various convenient locations and a fifth wireless long-range phone to take to the pool. The irony is that on any given day, a visit to the pool will reveal portable phone antennas protruding from many of the cabanas—and one cabana is merely calling its neighboring cabana!

The Four Seasons story is a perfect illustration of the fact that hotel design must take into account some crucial elements of modern human behavior: with few exceptions, we don't change our lifestyle when we change our location, and when it comes to communication, we want to keep our options open. Although we may not avail ourselves of the opportunity to stay constantly connected via phone or the Internet, we cling to the notion that if we wanted to, we could.

SHOWER THE PEOPLE

There are other design red flags. For example, the more a hotel loads up your room with amenities, the greater the likelihood that it's a badly designed room. This is simply another attempt to disguise the room's lack of functionality.

I have an admission to make: I have one of the world's largest international collections of designer and wannabe designer soaps and shampoos, all courtesy of hotels. There was one point about ten years ago when you couldn't check into a hotel without counting at least twelve individual branded products intended for each guest. However, designer soap won't rescue a badly designed or poorly functioning bathroom.

Like many people, I have one criterion to determine that a hotel is great: the shower in the bathroom—how big it is and how strong the water pressure is. That's what counts to me.

Many hotel rooms today still have puny showerheads, and the problem is compounded by bathtub faucets with badly working (or completely nonfunctional) antiscalding valves and redirector faucets. This results in low water pressure and no temperature control—you could easily be scalded by dripping water! In the first Travel Detective book, I mentioned booster pumps, which hotels put on different floors to maintain better water pressure. These pumps make a huge difference, and it's not a bad idea at check-in to ask the front desk clerk to call engineering and find out on which floors the hotel has installed these booster pumps. You want to book a room on one of those floors.

Though many hotels run hot and cold with their showers, there are some very pleasant surprises. The Savoy Hotel in London features giant, sixteen-inch-diameter stainless steel showerheads in its two hundred bathrooms. These showerheads are suspended from the ceiling rather than mounted on the wall, and the hotel's special supplemental water pressure system pumps water through narrow-gauge pipes at sixty-eight pounds per square inch. In fact, so many visitors like the showerheads that the hotel sells them on request.

What about temperature governors? I discovered my first many years ago at the Takaragaike Prince Hotel in Kyoto. I quickly learned that I could turn the faucet until it reaches a red line, at which point the water temperature is hot and steamy but bearable. If you want the shower hotter, you firmly depress a small red button on the faucet.

Shower temperature regulators can now also be found at many three-, four-, and five-star hotels around the world. At the Park Hyatt in Washington, a mixing valve prevents water from ever getting hotter than 130 degrees. At the Hyatt Regency in Honolulu, a similar "balancing spool" keeps the water temperature below 130 degrees, and an antiscalding device prevents sudden temperature fluctuations if the toilet is flushed while someone is in the shower.

In the United States and Europe, many older hotels, even after expensive renovations, still have a problem with water pressure. At the InterContinental in Paris, guests in rooms higher than the third floor often find themselves either too hot or too cold during their early morning showers. Local municipal codes notwithstanding (and, of course, I'm being environmentally incorrect here), I'm looking for a showerhead that shoots water out at the rate of twelve gallons a minute!

Surprisingly, the worst showers are often found at resort hotels, where it seems they spend more money on the outside environment than on the bathrooms. Despite special booster pumps, the Hyatt Regency in Maui suffers from chronic water pressure problems. The hotel is the last one on its stretch of beach to get its water, and the pressure suffers accordingly.

There are exceptions to this axiom about bad water pressure at resort hotels. At the Hilton Hawaiian Village in Honolulu, special rebooster systems have been installed for the thirty-five-story towers. And one of the nicer shower surprises can be found in southern Brittany, in the French resort city of La Baule. Dozens of little hotels line the beach facing the Atlantic, and most of them offer tiny rooms and even smaller bathrooms. But the thirty-room Castel Marie-Louise is exceptional—its showers have possibly the highest water pressure and consistency of temperature of any I've experienced. The smallness of the room was more than compensated for by the invigorating nature of the shower. I hate to say it, but the shower in that hotel was the highlight of my trip.

DO THE BEDS BUG YOU?

Of course, the most persistently loud guest complaints are about the hotel beds and bedding. Getting a good night's rest at a hotel is no easy task. How well you function on the road and at a hotel depends on how much you exercise, as well as how much and how well you sleep.

Hilton Hotels and Resorts commissioned the first-ever scientific study of its kind with a volunteer group of travelers to determine how travel impacts performance. Hilton fielded the two-month study, along with an extensive online survey, in cooperation with Dr. Mark Rosekind, a former director of NASA's Fatigue Countermeasures Program and current president of Alertness Solutions, a California-based scientific consulting firm.

As part of the research, participants wore wrist actigraphs that measured daytime activity levels and sleep quality and quantity. In addition, they carried special personal digital assistants (PDAs) that measured performance and served as a log for capturing details about their productivity, moods, and other daily rituals.

Not surprisingly, the study suggests that one of the primary reasons performance wanes is sleep loss. For example, study participants slept on average only five hours the night before a trip, the lowest of the entire seven-day monitoring period. Any sleep period of less than six hours a night begins to significantly diminish performance, Rosekind reported. "Essentially, travelers are at a decreased productivity level before they even walk out their door."

In all, study participants registered a total sleep loss of almost eight hours by the time they returned home, the equivalent of one full night's sleep. That's a finding scientists say has broader implications than just performance.

The obvious implication of the study is that the hotel sleep experience should be the most important aspect of any stay, so it's surprising that hotels don't pay more attention to their beds.

The hotel room bed is perhaps the one great unknown for the traveler. No hyperbolic advertisement or glossy brochure—or even this book—can adequately guarantee you a great bed at a hotel. Nevertheless, certain things can be determined. It may come as a surprise, but many hotels still order institutional-quality beds for guest rooms—and, in some cases, the quality of these beds is marginal. Some hotel beds contain the same spring units that the United States uses in government hospital beds—or worse.

However, not everyone is an institutional-quality guest. At one hotel in Chicago, a frequent guest, who happens to be a former NBA star, performs a regular bedtime ritual: he pulls up two armchairs, drops the standard mattress, and stuffs four to six extra pillows between the headboard and the mattress to accommodate his six-foot, eight-inch height. In this case, the hotel can be excused for its failure to provide an adequate bed. But what about more typical guests?

Many hotel guests now anticipate the worst and ask for a bedboard as mattress support when they check in. If you're like me, you'll find many hotel beds so uncomfortable that you'll be forced to go on pillow patrol, rounding up extra pillows to compensate for an unforgiving mattress.

There are exceptions, of course. Not every expensive hotel will have great beds, and not every budget hotel bed will send you to an orthopedic surgeon. For example, the Westin Heavenly Bed has been extremely popular with guests. Many people sleep in one once and decide they want to buy one (they can).

Overseas, nowhere is the subject of the hotel beds taken more seriously than at the Savoy in London. The hotel can boast that it literally makes its own mattresses and box springs.

The Savoy owns its own upholstery business and has a factory off Drury Lane. A special team of three people produces just 420 mattresses a year, and they are very special indeed: each single mattress has 836 springs and consists of sixteen pounds of horsehair, thirty-one pounds of lambswool, and a heavy wooden frame, into which a hand-sewn linen casing, specially woven in County Armagh, Ireland, is placed.

All of the Savoy's mattresses are six feet, six inches long, a good three inches longer than most U.S. beds. The average life span of each Savoy mattress is twenty-five years. However, every ten years the mattresses are returned to the factory for reconditioning.

The individually handmade mattresses have become so popular that many guests have asked to buy them. As a result, the Savoy sells, crates, and ships its custom-made mattresses across the Atlantic. However, the true test of a great hotel bed often depends less on the type of bed than it does on how the hotel staff maintains it (see Chapter 7).

Among my favorites are the beds at the Four Seasons, which

are made under special contract with Sealy. They are some of the most comfortable I've ever experienced—so comfortable, in fact, that I bought four of them for my house. And I'm not alone: Oprah Winfrey purchased eleven (she's got a bigger house).

After my house was destroyed in the 1994 California earthquake, I decided to apply many of the design lessons I had learned from hotels—both aesthetic and practical—to the new house I was building. By the time I was finished, I had constructed a state-of-the-art but *comfortable* house from the combined design principles used in forty-seven separate hotels. The floors originated at the Sheraton in Stockholm, the privacy windows were like those at the Princeville Resort in Kauai, and the kitchen was based on the one in the Mark Hotel in New York. The toilets replicated those at the Park Hyatt in Tokyo, the phone system was borrowed from the Sheraton in Buenos Aires, and the cabinet knobs and sinks copied those at the Europa and Regina in Venice. The showerhead, of course, came from the Savoy!

The important concept here is that when hotel design and function actually work, you should take advantage of them. Just about everything but the original artwork is for sale at your hotel, even though there is no price tag hanging on it. All the things I bought for my house are accessible to anyone. As hotels get smarter about design and try to re-create or even improve on our own homes and aesthetic styles, you might find that you like something in your hotel so much that you decide to buy it and ship it home.

DESIGNERS ON DESIGN

I asked two hotel designers, Dan Nelson—author of my favorite "hotels are hospitals with better carpets" quote—and Patrick Burke, who designs hotels with the legendary Michael Graves, to think like guests and tell me the things they both hate and love about most hotel rooms. So the next time you check into a hotel for the first time, you can use their checklists of red-flag items— things to look for that are warning signs of bad design, as well as things that strongly indicate the hotel was actually thinking about you, the guest. First, Dan Nelson's indicators of bad hotel design:

- Ineffective or no signage. You know it is bad when you walk into a hotel and can't tell which desk is for check-in.

- Depressing corridors with bad lighting. This is not a good way to start a hotel stay.

- Draperies that are on old-fashioned drawstrings instead of "flick sticks" that you can grab to move the curtains. It is a nuisance to hunt for the drawstrings and not be able to tell the sheer from the curtain, and then pull them the wrong way.

- No radios or CD players.

- Huge armoires that are out of scale to the rooms. These usually house the TV, minibar, fax machine, stereo, and CD player, in addition to drawers for holding belongings. All they need are wheels and you could call them Winnebagos.

- Lack of or bad placement of outlets to plug in computers, cell phones, and other portable electronic equipment.

- Bad fluorescent lighting. (Is there such a thing as good fluorescent lighting?)

- Showers that are part of the bathtub. A walk-in shower and no tub would be preferable. Although hotels still seem to think they have to install tubs, they are rarely used.

- Recessed lights over the bed that shine in your eyes.

According to Nelson, every good hotel room should incorporate these features:

- Attractive and appropriate linens. This is what you are there for, after all. The duvet look is appealing, but rooms should also have a blanket stashed somewhere in a drawer or closet. Good-quality pillows are likewise a must! Many people actually travel with their own pillows because hotel pillows are notoriously inadequate.

- A comfortable place to sit or have sex other than the bed. (It's easy to lose sight of the fact that hotels are subliminally selling sex.)

- An iron and ironing board or good butler service.

- Thoughtfully planned air-conditioning, which includes easily controlled thermostats and vents that do not blow directly on the bed.

- Ample counter space in the bathroom, even if it means having one sink instead of two.

- Sexy faucet and shower sets with good showerheads that deliver sufficient flow to rinse your hair.

- Full-length mirrors.

- Adequate sound abatement, particularly from the hallways.

- A room safe big enough for a laptop computer.

- Well-thought-out lighting, including good reading lamps with three-way switches to give guests more control and help set the mood when they are turned down.

- Adequate blackout capability at the windows.

On the basis of aesthetics rather than practicality, Nelson gives a negative nod to the W in New York (the one I had the problem with). "I upgraded to a suite my first visit," Nelson reports, "and the sofa in the tiny living room was covered in white linen. I can imagine that the look was good the first day or so, but by the time I got there things had been done on that sofa that I did not want to know about. They also had benches with built-in shallow planters at one end. They had been planted with some sort of decorative short cropped grass. About half of them had been sat on, probably in some drunken stupor. I am sure that there are still some people trying to figure out how they got grass stains on their asses!"

THE SHREK HONEYMOON SUITE:
Universal Studios Hollywood and the Sheraton Universal have created the Shrek Honeymoon Suite. This luxury room comes complete with living area, breakfast nook, and king-size bed reminiscent of Shrek's lodging in the animated movie. Nestled within a forestlike atmosphere, the suite opens with a hand-painted, heart-shaped doorway and is totally "shrekked out" from floor to ceiling and from bed to bath.

Patrick Burke, who just completed a major guest room redesign at the Swan and the Dolphin hotels at the Walt Disney World Resorts in Lake Buena Vista, Florida, has his own list of problems with hotel design.

First, he contends, it's all about color and functionality. So many hotel rooms are cut from the same cookie-cutter mold. These hotels do not seem to know how to recognize or honor the particular environment they are in by incorporating it as a design theme. They use identical overpatterned fabrics and carpeting that declare their adherence to a "grandma aesthetic." When I see rooms like this it's obvious that the designers use lots of the color red to hide ketchup stains. Rooms that use an abundance of bad paisleys and florals have only one goal: to mask dirt and stains.

HOTEL ON ICE: At the Ice Hotel in Jukkasjärvi, Sweden, visitors are pleased to freeze. There's an old Scandinavian saying, "There's no such thing as cold weather, only bad clothing," so the hotel provides padded suits, gloves, thermal boots, and warm reindeer skins. Some people prefer a spell in the sun, but the Ice Hotel has proved very popular with pop stars, supermodels, politicians, and royalty checking in and chilling out.

The amount of space is not the only consideration, either. Marriott Courtyard Hotels offer big rooms, but they use the space poorly. Hotel owners and designers must employ some common sense when designing rooms to ensure that no odd pieces of furniture or molding protrude into the traffic pattern. It is also wise to design a bathroom block, so that guests who are not familiar with the room layout can easily find the bathroom in the dark.

Such basic design principles seem intuitive, yet they aren't incorporated often enough. The most likely reason for this is that the hotel corporation picks out a block of furniture, and then the design team has to make it work. The two teams are not working together from the beginning, as they should.

Nevertheless, limitations can be the inspiration for new designs. Disney's designers are good at those details, such as avoiding sharp edges on furnishings. They also dislike using anything that potentially could show dirt. For example, they will put a desk against the wall and use a backsplash—not exactly a design coup, but it's easier to clean.

Disney is now bringing in outside designers and moving away from the traditional Disney theme and characters. They want to be kid-friendly but also target adults. In fact, 80 percent of Disney's hotel business consists of adult business and convention travelers. Therefore, in updating the room design ten years after opening, Patrick Burke wanted to address the needs of the business traveler as well as those of families, update the interior aesthetically and functionally, make the rooms more domestic and comfortable, and rethink some of the details of those rooms. He considered the following aspects in his design process.

- *Colors and patterns.* The original Dolphin and Swan rooms relied on multicolored elements, boldly patterned fabrics and furniture, and whimsical graphic icons to convey the energy and spirit of the Walt Disney World context. In the updated rooms, he simplified and lightened the color scheme, reduced the patterns, and eliminated the whimsical icons. The new color scheme uses warm creams and ochre in lighter values, a simply patterned terra-cotta-colored carpet and light blue curtain, and white bed linens and duvet cover. The room appears simpler and warmer than before, and the lighter colors make it feel somewhat larger.

- *Furniture.* Burke reduced the number of pieces of furniture to make the room feel more spacious, enhance functionality, and improve the guest's comfort. All new furniture is finished in a light honey-stained maple to replace the original multicolored furniture. This contributes to the lighter, warmer, "quieter" room design and keeps the feel of these rooms unified. The furniture has light turquoise glass in the recesses to add gentle contrast and sparkle. The glass tops of the original tables, which were showing wear and tear after years of use, are replaced by light slate-blue laminate tops for durability and a cool color contrast to the prevailing warm tones.

One major change to the furniture is the use of the new Heavenly Bed. The other major change was replacing the desk (which was too small for a convention guest needing to work in the room) and the large TV armoire (which was the norm at the time) with a ten-foot-long all-in-one unit with a more appealing and modern-looking TV on top, dresser drawers, and a long desk space on which to spread out work. Eliminating the armoire made the room feel much more spacious and allows guests to watch TV from the desk, which was impossible before. A large circular mirror, five feet in diameter, hangs above the all-in-one unit, which increases the sense of spaciousness and adds to the quality of light in the room.

• *Art.*   The design of the original rooms was very active, and Burke therefore made the artwork rather simple. Since the new rooms are visually much quieter, he was able to use the artwork to make a bolder statement. He used large prints of Michael Graves's "archaic landscape" paintings above the headboards to accomplish this. These landscapes are all 2.5 feet high and range in length from 4.5 to 6 feet long. These help create a special atmosphere, since they appear as large paintings rather than framed posters.

As a designer, Burke finds the following hotel features most annoying:

• Rooms with that "lowest common denominator" appearance that are not only boring but look like they were designed by a consortium of opinions offered by the housekeeping administration, focus groups, budget experts, and businesspeople who rely on playing it safe rather than achieving superior quality. Such hotels could have come off an assembly line. They are generic in experience and ultimately lifeless. Guests should have higher expectations for the room quality, experience and style, given the rates they are paying.

- Guest room layouts where the furniture interferes with traffic patterns.

- Bad furniture layouts. Usually this is a result of having too much furniture, the wrong furniture, or the wrong idea of what a guest room should be like.

- Bathroom countertops with no place to put *my* stuff. This frustration is doubled when traveling as a couple and there is no place for *our* stuff.

- Air-conditioning units that keep you awake all night. (Earplugs should not really have to be part of the amenity package!)

- Walls that do not separate the guest rooms acoustically. It's no fun spending a night in a hotel either listening to someone else's TV preferences or getting more involved in someone else's life than you would like.

- Light switches that cannot be reached from the bed.

- Desks sized for a second-grader.

- Desks oriented so you cannot watch TV when you are sitting there.

Here is Burke's wish list (and, come to think of it, mine, too) for a well-designed hotel:

- A room produced by a good designer, which has a real sense of style and is unique to the particular place where the hotel is located. This gives guests the feeling that they are staying somewhere special and participating in the local character of their destination.

- Good, comfortable beds with good-quality linens.

- Real showers.

- Enough counter space in the bathroom for stuff. And, for women, sufficient lighting to apply makeup.

- TV locations that are visible from the bed, desk, and any sofas or lounge chairs. Someone who stays there for several days will probably be watching TV from every location in the room at one time or another.

- Quiet heating, ventilation, and air-conditioning systems.

- Light switches within reaching distance of the bed.

- Rooms that really do have enough light at the bed for reading.

- Closets deep enough to hold a hanging suitcase. (Here's an additional tip from me: if you want to steam your clothes on the shower curtain rod in the bathroom, remember that those little hooks on the hangers in the closet won't fit around the rod. Many of my friends now travel with at least one sturdy wooden coat hanger, which they use for that purpose.)

- A desk large enough to spread out work.

CHAPTER 7

What the Housekeepers Won't Tell You

A recent survey asked travelers what hotel services they'd most like to have in their own homes. By an overwhelming margin of 64 percent, the travelers voted for maid service. Only 3 percent said they wanted to find a mint on their pillow at home.

And why wouldn't you want maid service? It's the best amenity. You wouldn't want to *be* the maid, however. They are, without doubt, the hardest-working people at hotels. They are the true unsung and underappreciated heroes of the business.

When it comes to the subject of hotel sanitation and cleanliness and the staff who perform these duties, most hoteliers like to talk in general philosophic terms about such things as corporate goals, mission statements, and, yes, good intentions. But details are not forthcoming. It is a very touchy subject—and not necessarily a feel-good one. It's somewhat ironic that a number of hotels have now stopped putting Gideon Bibles in guest rooms at the very time when we might need them the most—to pray for a truly clean room! But before you blame the maids, read on.

I always thought the procedure went like this: the maid came into my room, changed the sheets and pillowcases, vacuumed, dusted, and waxed the furniture. In the bathroom, she (or he, although most cleaning staffs are female) thoroughly scrubbed the toilet, bathtub, and sink and replaced the drinking glasses with new, sterilized ones. For years, I arrived at hotel rooms expecting to see the toilet seat wrapped with a thin strip of paper announcing that it had been "sanitized for your protection." Then in the late afternoon or early evening, another maid entered to turn the bed down and, if I was particularly lucky, put some chocolate or a mint on the pillow.

Well, that's a nice, sentimental thought. But today, more often than not, these things don't quite happen that way.

> **CRY FOR HELP:** A hotel notice in Madrid informs guests: "If you wish disinfection enacted in your presence, please cry out for the chambermaid."

First, consider what it means to be a hotel maid. Imagine being told that your job definition is to clean sixteen rooms a day, with only two 15-minute breaks on an eight-hour shift. That works out to just slightly more than 23 minutes to clean each room. To complicate matters, people you don't know, often with questionable hygiene habits, occupy each room; many are slobs. Their existence expands to fill the space they're given. They smoke. They drink. They have sex. Some have pets. And some, well, are animals themselves—both when they occupy the rooms and then, later, when they check out.

If a hotel has more checkouts than check-ins on a given day, and the people checking out are tourists or shoppers, then the rooms they've left will most likely be filled with clutter that must be removed before you can begin cleaning—all of which must still be taken care of in just twenty-three minutes. That's not a lot of time. In fact, it's clearly not enough time to get the rooms clean.

When it comes to the cleanliness of a hotel room, it's important that the room look good. However, it's much more important that the room actually is *clean*. This is a challenge that few hotels meet.

Think of everything you physically come in contact with in a hotel room: doorknobs, carpet, bedspread, bathroom floor, sheets, pillows, blankets, drinking glasses, telephones, TV remote control unit, sink, toilet, and bathtub or shower. How clean are they? (Hint: It's a rhetorical question.)

I have to warn you: this isn't pretty. Years ago, I did blacklight tests on hotel bedspreads and carpets. Additional chemical analysis revealed more than just traces of urine, semen, pubic hair, saliva, and blood. And this was *after* the rooms had presumably been cleaned.

But the situation is actually worse than that. Begin with the premise that maids are overburdened. Add to that the fact of staffing cuts in a downward economy, even at union hotels, which means the number of maids is at a minimum. When maids rush through their shifts—as they must—they either miss stuff entirely or do a very hasty job of camouflage. As a result, I've checked into dozens of rooms where seeing is . . . deceiving. Furniture isn't dusted. Mirrors aren't clean. And, of course, there's always the dreaded bedspread to contend with.

Then there's the myth of the nonsmoking rooms. Such rooms do exist, but in reality, not for long. Why? Even smokers will tell you they ask for them. It's easy to recognize in a matter of seconds that the previous guest has smoked in the room. Also, when you enter a room for the first time and detect a distinctly sweet floral or soapy smell, chances are that the maids have attempted to cover the traces of the last smoking guest by doing some heavy spraying.

FASTEST HANDS IN THE EAST: A chambermaid at the Helmsley Windsor Hotel won the Fastest Hands in the East contest by making three beds in three minutes and thirty-seven seconds. She was awarded a Miami Beach vacation and $500.

Whenever there is a particularly bad odor that lingers in a room, hotels bring in ozone-generating machines to try to neutralize it, in addition to using that obnoxious spray. The problem is that, if not properly monitored, ozone generation in high concentrations can cause respiratory problems. It has been estimated that a standard guest room can be deodorized in thirty minutes with two hundred milligrams per hour of ozone. However, the stronger the contamination, the more ozone you need.

And I don't care what anyone says—that smell just won't go away. I know people who actually carry their own potpourri to hotels! There's a simpler solution: ask to move to a different room.

GOOD HOUSEKEEPING

You can—and should—control the cleanliness of certain areas of your hotel room.

- *Bedspreads.* In the first Travel Detective book, I advised that you take off the bedspread immediately upon checking in. That advice still holds. Hotels hardly ever clean bedspreads—it's as simple as that. So remove it.

- *TVs and telephones.* I now also advise bringing some Handi Wipes with you to concentrate on two specific areas that maids do not clean: TV remote control units, which consistently carry high levels of bacteria, and telephone handsets, many of which need thorough cleaning of the ear- and mouthpieces.

- *Pillows.* Ask the housekeeping department to send up three additional pillows. Take the existing pillows off the bed and put them in the closet. As for the pillow that's already in the closet, there's an excellent chance that it's cleaner than the original pillows on the bed, so you can actually use that one as a fourth pillow. In my experience, unless you travel with your own pillows, you can never have enough.

- *Beds.* Sometimes it's actually *how* the bed is made that can make a huge difference in the quality of the sleep you get during your hotel experience. For example, the Mandarin Oriental in Hong Kong uses a special method of folding the sheets on the beds, which has been nicknamed "the Bangkok Fold." The practice was started at the legendary Oriental Hotel in Bangkok, and it's really quite simple: the maid puts an extra fold in the sheet at the base of the bed, which allows for free movement of the feet. It's amazing the difference that makes.

DID THE BEDBUGS LEAVE THE LIGHT ON FOR YOU?? A federal appeals court in Washington let stand an original jury award of $372,000 in punitive damages against a Chicago hotel that had continued to rent bedbug-infested rooms. The Motel 6 on East Ontario Street (which is now operated as a Red Roof Inn) actually admitted during the original trial that it knew of the bedbug infestation—and still did nothing to fix the problem. One of the things that apparently won the case: an appeals court judge kept noting that the hotel refused to have the entire property exterminated for only $500.

- *Ice buckets.*   Never use ice directly from the ice bucket; always use the plastic liner. They never clean the ice buckets.

- *Coffeepots.*   Generally speaking, most hotels do not wash the in-room coffeepots and cups, they merely rinse and wipe them out.

- *Towels.*   I remember staying at the Hilton Hotel in Springfield, Illinois, where the towels in the bathroom were the size of loincloths. To add insult to injury, there was a plastic tent card placed on the sink announcing that if you took the towel, you'd be charged $7. I couldn't stop laughing. The towels were unusable to begin with! So I stopped a maid in the hall as she completed her rounds and asked her how many people stole those towels. She laughed, "No one." I told her I couldn't believe they even called them towels. She smiled and said she could solve my problem. In some of the suites, the hotel provided bath sheets, and she got me two, so I tipped her. And this is good advice. Indeed, many hotels provision their suites with nicer towels than are provided in rooms. Often they also supply bathrobes. Ask the maid nicely, tip her, and she will take care of you.

- *Dusty surfaces.*   If you're allergic to animals, make sure to ask whether there were pets in your room anytime in the past thirty days (see the section in Chapter 13 on pet-friendly hotels). Most maids do not dust above armoires or other high furniture and objects—in many cases, they don't even *look* up there. You'd be surprised by what some people leave on the top of armoires—everything from used condoms (don't even ask how they got up there) to beer bottles and the telltale ashtray with cigarette butts the previous guest tried to hide.

- *Carpets.*   Do not walk around barefoot. Remember what I said about hotels intentionally installing heavily patterned carpets to mask dirt and stains? Either bring a pair of your own slippers or, if the hotel provides them, wear a pair of theirs.

The next stop is the bathroom. Now it's going to get truly ugly.

- *Drinking Glasses.*   Hotel-supplied drinking glasses may look clean, but there's a good chance the maid didn't replace them after the last guest checked out. More likely, she gave them a cursory rinse in the sink, wiped them dry, and returned them to the bathroom.

- *Bathtubs.*   If a maid is running late, she may not clean the bathtub at all. Instead, she's likely to grab a towel, wet it, and do one quick wipe or "pat down." That's it. Although it may waste water, as a precaution before taking a bath, fill the tub to see what's floating around, then drain it, and wipe it out yourself.

- *Shower curtains.*   This is another breeding ground for bacteria and mold. In some bathrooms, hotels use vinyl liners with overlay shower curtains. The curtains themselves are hardly ever cleaned, and if the vinyl liners aren't cleaned, mold grows.

Marriott recently audited its hotels and discovered a disturbing statistic: in the eight hundred hotels it checked, one in four Marriott guests had a problem with the guest room. The problems were found in two areas. The first was TV remote control units that didn't work because a previous guest took the battery to operate another portable electronic device or due to some malfunction in the unit itself.

The other problem was in the bathroom, where good intentions seemed to be backfiring. In an effort to be environmentally friendly, numerous Marriott hotels (and this is also happening at other hotels) have been retrofitting their rooms with low-flush toilets, which use about half the water to flush as the old models. That's the good news. The bad news is they often don't flush completely. To compensate for this, when maids clean the bathrooms, they are supposed to flush the toilets—and generally they do. However, sometimes they forget to check after they flush. The result is that a growing number of guests, either returning to their rooms or checking in for the first time, discover a rather unwelcome surprise waiting for them in the bathroom.

THE GREEN HOTEL ROOM DILEMMA

In this world of political correctness, I must admit to some serious cynicism—especially when it comes to those little tent cards placed in bedrooms and bathrooms that encourage us not to have our sheets changed or our washcloths and towels laundered "for the sake of the environment."

I understand the environmental impact of phosphates, but, please, if I'm paying $150 a night for my room, I want clean sheets, clean towels, and clean washcloths. Many hotels that claim to be environmentally friendly are doing nothing more than obeying municipal codes and expecting us to thank them for it.

A placard found in a Denver Hyatt guest room read as follows:

> As mandated by Denver Board of Water commissioner and as part of Hyatt's ongoing commitment to improve the environment by using less energy and creating less waste, we offer a solution. During your stay, we will change the bed linens and towels every four days, while still refreshing your guestroom daily. If you do not wish to participate in this program, please contact "Perfect Stay" at extension 36 or the hotel operator and your linens and towels will be replaced daily.

I had to laugh at the words "Perfect Stay." I called someone in management there to make sure I got the service I thought I was already paying for. (At the Denver Hyatt, the bedspreads are cleaned only every other month—that's definitely not being friendly to *my* environment.)

According to the National Association of Institutional Linen Management (yes, there really is such an organization), average per-room laundry costs range from $3 to $4 per day. Some industry experts now estimate that hotels can save about

$2 per day per room by not washing and replacing towels and sheets every day in every room.

So the next time you're confronted with the "green" hotel request not to launder your towels, why not ask for a $2-per-night reduction in your room rate, just on principle?

If hotels really want to help the environment, they should get rid of all unnecessary paper products, including promotional tent cards. They should install low-cost sink aerators and 2.5-gallon-per-minute showerheads, use coreless toilet paper rolls, put halogen lamps at the work desks, and supply unwrapped soap. In the guest bedrooms, they should use organic cotton bedding. Cleaning agents should not contain disinfectants. The housekeeping department should replace vacuum cleaner bags with reusable cloth ones. They should turn mattresses every ninety days and use linens with a higher thread count. Installing magnetic latches on patio doors cuts down on the air-conditioning or heat that escapes when the doors are opened.

One Toronto hotel is recycling stained tablecloths into napkins, chef's aprons, and ties. Other hotels are making laundry bags out of retired sheets. And a growing number of hotels are exploring alternative energy sources, such as solar power and power generated from the wind.

Nevertheless, let's not carry this too far. I do not like fluorescent lightbulbs. They may save on electricity costs, but hotel guests are slowly going blind from the harshness of the light they put out. One friend of mine, a frequent business traveler, actually carries two 100-watt bulbs with him on every trip.

> **MILES OF LAUNDRY:** The Las Vegas Hilton washes forty-two thousand pounds of laundry daily, including eight thousand sheets, which, if laid end to end, would be more than thirteen miles long.

And don't wire rooms so that the master switch controls any outlet near the work desk—I need my laptop to charge even when I'm not in the room. All too often, I leave my room, turn off the master switch by the door, and in the process drain my computer's battery. If the hotel where you are staying wires the master switch that way, leave a note taped to the switch telling the maid to leave it in the permanent "on" position.

And then, since hotels are saving so much money from these environmentally friendly practices, they can supply me with fresh towels and sheets every day!

A STITCH IN TIME: Park Plaza Hotel cleaning supervisor and seamstress Odette Daher might not consider herself an environmentalist, but her elegant needlework — turning old bedspreads and linen tablecloths with cigarette burns into fashionable aprons and plush stuffed animals — is a featured part of the greening of the once-staid Boston, Massachusetts, establishment.

Here's my handy tip for checking whether the maids actually vacuum your room and change the sheets. If you're staying at a hotel for more than one night, do the following: before you leave your room, pull back the covers on the bed, tear out a match from a matchbook, and place it on top of the bottom sheet at the foot of the bed. Then pull the sheets back up. Take a second match and place it on the carpet directly under, parallel, and even with the edge of the bed. When you return to the room, if the match is still on the carpet, the room wasn't properly vacuumed. Pull back the blanket and sheets. If the match is still at the end of the bed, then the sheets weren't changed.

ALL THAT YOU LEAVE BEHIND

Maids are often the only ones who see hotel rooms while they are occupied. And they're also the first to discover the myriad of items, many of them surprises, that guests leave behind in their rooms when they check out.

I saw it as soon I entered the room in my New York hotel. Sitting in the corner on the floor was a pink fabric purse. Inside were half a dozen rings and pendants, and a pearl necklace. I called the front desk and told them of my discovery. Less than five minutes later a plainclothes security officer was at my door. He had brought along another officer to act as a witness while he inventoried the contents of the purse and recorded my name, the date, and the time. A week later a woman who had been a guest at the hotel claimed the purse. She was not only amazed that the purse had been found (she had dropped it on her way to check out) but astounded that it had been returned.

This woman was lucky. Thousands of items are left in hotels each year by guests, and most are never recovered or returned. In some cases the guest doesn't want the item, but often, when the person realizes the item is missing, he or she assumes it is lost forever. This is not necessarily true.

If you were to examine the contents of the lost-and-found department of an average hotel, here is what you would be most likely to find: jewelry, cameras, hair dryers, cologne, perfume, makeup, shaving supplies, nightgowns, pajamas, undergarments, credit cards, hats, shoes, and books.

The numbers might surprise you. Most major city hotels and resorts report about five thousand items being turned in to their lost-and-found departments. At one Arizona hotel, the booty includes everything from six sets of false teeth to diamond rings and a now-famous stuffed chicken.

Whether it's a hair dryer or $150,000 worth of jewelry that was left behind in your room, you should file a found property

SHINE ON: Dorothy Raybon works at the Chicago Ritz-Carlton, a hotel that offers guests a special service. Place your shoes in the hallway by 1 A.M., and they will be returned good as new by 6 A.M. Most nights, Raybon shines about fifty or sixty pairs. But some nights, especially in the winter or after a heavy rain, she shines more than a hundred. The hotel has about four hundred rooms and seventeen floors, so it takes Raybon several hours just to pick up each pair. The hotel has an automatic machine, but Raybon says she prefers to do it by hand.

"I'm just as fast," she says.

report, including any information that is known about the item and/or its owner. In some cases it might be difficult for the owner to make an exact identification of an item. In the case of the stuffed chicken (not the kind delivered by room service but the kind handled by a taxidermist) that was left behind, the owner had not been located after the mandatory six-month waiting period. Stuffed-chicken lovers will be relieved to know that the chicken was given a new home.

While in London recently, I asked to see the inventory of a major hotel's lost-and-found department. A three-month collection of items that had been left behind or lost included dozens of undergarments, prescription drugs, eyeglasses, a rubber sheet, a pair of pliers, casino chips, and some videocassettes.

The value of an item is not always obvious. One woman who left her hot-water bottle insisted on getting it back, claiming it had tremendous sentimental value. At the Plaza in New York, what appeared to be an old, tattered, and frayed nightgown turned out to be the garment that the woman wore on her wedding night fifty years earlier at the same hotel.

Sometimes guests lose things but prefer not to admit that they have lost them. That's why most hotels practice discretion.

When a hotel maid finds something that a guest left behind in a room, the hotel often contacts the departed guest by sending a vague letter that says, "We think you may have left something behind," and asks the guest to contact the hotel.

> **SIGN OF THE TIMES:** Jean Francois Vernetti, a Swiss accountant, holds the record for the largest collection of "Do Not Disturb" signs. Collecting signs since 1985, he now has 2,915 from 131 different countries. "Every sign brings back a special memory," Says Vernetti, who now never stays in the same hotel twice—just so he can add more signs to his collection.

A few years ago the maids at the Halekulani Hotel in Honolulu found a pair of black leopard-print panties, a family-size bottle of Klausen's pickles, and a marriage certificate that a guest had left behind. No one ever claimed them. But if you're reading this and you got married in Hawaii, and sexy lingerie and pickles were involved, don't call me—call the Halekulani. The hotel will gladly send them back to you, no questions asked.

What item is left in hotel rooms most frequently? Cell phone chargers. Here's a tip: if you left your charger at your last hotel, just call the lost-and-found at your *next* hotel and ask whether they have your model in *their* lost-and-found. Odds are very strong that another guest will have lost the same model, and you can save yourself some trouble by borrowing it to charge your phone.

The second most frequently left behind item is womens' watches—and there seems to be a logical explanation for this: women often travel with more than one watch. And third, but never least, are sexual devices and lingerie. In this case, it's probably *not* a good idea to call downstairs to ask whether they have, uh, your "model."

CHAPTER 8

What the Concierge
Won't Tell You

It has been said that one machine can do the work of fifty ordinary people. No machine, however, can do the work of one *extraordinary* person.

Consider the story of Olivier, the legendary concierge at the Ritz Hotel in Paris. In 1900, his guests were counts and countesses, barons and baronesses. To deny one of these people a request or a whim was unthinkable. One of his guests was the Marquise Casati, who frequently arrived at the hotel with her pet boa constrictor. The large snake ate nothing but live rabbits, which was bad enough. But the marquise also brought with her a hooded falcon, which favored live pigeons. Olivier thought nothing of asking whether the falcon preferred any particular breed of pigeon. And he supplied both rabbits and special pigeons every time she stayed there.

Today, more than one hundred years later, nothing much has changed with the concierges at the Ritz. While everyone in the hotel business talks about new concepts of service and empowerment, there's still really only one hotel staffer who has personified these concepts for years: the concierge.

Ever wonder what a hotel concierge really does? The answer is: just about everything. A great concierge starts with an encyclopedic memory and adds a limitless supply of energy, impressive multilingual skills, and an unequaled ability to successfully work any network to fulfill guest requests. Whether you want dinner reservations, transportation, sightseeing tips, or advice, the concierge can arrange it. And that's just the beginning.

A concierge, once a fixture exclusive to old-world European hotels, is now very much a part of many U.S. hotels. The true concierge is, at the very least, a hotel miracle worker—a man (or woman) with all the best connections. Sometimes, the concierge is the person with the *only* connections. More often than not, a good concierge functions as a human Rolodex and is thus a hotel's most valuable player. As a result, few requests are too outrageous for good hotel concierges:

- A guest at the Four Seasons in Philadelphia wanted a better look at some property he was considering buying. The concierge arranged for him to be picked up by helicopter within an hour.

- One morning, a wealthy guest at the old Inn on the Park in Houston wanted to have a big party the same evening. He wanted to hold the party at a mansion, with a swimming pool and tennis courts. The concierge set it up in less than four hours.

- The concierge at the Hotel Crescent Court in Dallas received an urgent call from a guest at the hotel who also happened to be the president of an African country. His request: he needed the concierge to locate and secure a jumbo jet for a charter, whose departure was to take place in less than two hours. The concierge made two phone calls, found a DC-10 with the right configuration in New Orleans, and had the jet flown in and waiting at the airport in Dallas with several minutes to spare.

- A few years ago, the concierge at the Beverly Hills Hotel arranged an audience with the pope for a guest who was traveling to Rome.

It's all about connections. A good concierge is actually a cross between a bartender, a priest, and an inside fixer. Surprisingly, however, few guests, including business travelers, use concierges properly, or at all.

HOW DO YOU SPELL CONCIERGE?

Just because a hotel advertises it has a concierge doesn't mean you'll receive concierge service. In some cases, the "concierge" at your hotel may not truly be a concierge but a nattily attired bell captain wearing a set of gold-plated keys or a different gold-braid-trimmed uniform than the rest of the staff.

A hotel in Dallas once promoted itself with the slogan "let us astound you," announcing that as part of their new campaign to please guests they had initiated concierge service. The hotel pronounced their new concierge capable of great wizardry and proudly placed the concierge desk in the center of the lobby. Indeed, the concierge wasted no time astounding the guests. The concierge desk, as it turned out, was nothing more than an information desk staffed by an inexperienced employee. Not long thereafter, the concierge job was eliminated and the lobby desk was removed. It was replaced by a large plant.

It can be helpful to know a little something about the concierge at your hotel—how long he or she has been in the position and, perhaps more important, how long the concierge has worked, not at that particular hotel but in that city, which makes a big difference in how much you can trust the person's advice.

Recently a couple checked into one of New York's more expensive hotels and asked someone at the concierge desk to recommend a good Italian restaurant. Their only caveat was that it had to be a short cab ride away, because after dinner they wanted to walk back to the hotel. The concierge gave them the name of what he called a great Italian restaurant, supposedly five minutes away by cab, and told them he would take care of everything. A reservation was made for 8 P.M.

At 7:45, the couple left the hotel by cab. Twenty minutes later, they finally arrived at the restaurant. The place was in Greenwich Village, a good distance from the hotel, it was Greek, it took no reservations, and it didn't accept credit cards.

Needless to say, the couple didn't eat there, and they didn't exactly walk home.

When first-time guests find out that the concierge can't help them, they don't come back a second time. However, good hotel concierges place virtually no limits on their job definition, so don't be afraid to ask them if you need something, even if it seems impossible.

If you frequent particular hotels, it's probably more important to cultivate a relationship with the concierge than with any other employee. In fact, hotels rotate their general managers about five times more frequently than they replace their concierges.

The concierge at the Mandarin Oriental Hotel in Hong Kong, Giovanni Valenti, has been there more than twenty-five years. Everyone calls him Mr. Valenti. And there isn't an airline representative, shoe repairperson, luggage expert, tour operator, or Chinese junk captain who doesn't owe him at least one large favor.

Need an express visa to get into China? Ask Mr. Valenti. Did you buy too much to fit into your suitcase for the return trip home? Valenti will pack it for you. (In fact, the concierge staff constructs an average of thirty-five heavily reinforced packages a day for guests.) "I try very hard," he says, "to make sure that the word 'no' isn't in my vocabulary. At the very worst, I come up with a very good plan B."

In recent years, some guests have been surprised to find that many of the best hotel concierges are women. Years ago, the Hotel Royal Monceau in Paris, France, boasted the first female concierge in a French four-star hotel. Now many French hotels have women concierges.

Any concierge can ultimately find someone theater tickets, but, more important, good concierges must be diligent students of human values and resources. They must know manners, and they must know languages. If they can't speak to the guests, how can they do anything for them?

Valenti is part of a select group of hotel concierges who belong to Les Cles d'Or, the prestigious international organization of concierges. (In the United States there are only about 120 members of Les Cles d'Or.)

"Most people are intimidated by concierges," Valenti contends. "They are afraid of the word itself, and what they really do. They think only about what it will cost them, without realizing that a concierge is paid by the hotel and is a service that is already absorbed in the room cost."

"We are a dying breed," says Giorgio Finocchiaro, a legendary hotel concierge who now services private clients. For nearly fifteen years, Finocchiaro was the concierge at the Mark Hotel in New York. He was the magician, the alchemist, and the performer of impossible deeds and finisher of outrageous tasks.

"The problem today," he reports, "is technology and greed. People think technology can replace concierges, and what the technology doesn't destroy, greed will."

But at high-end hotels, concierges not only still exist, they reign supreme. If you want something done, the concierge is your person.

In Finocchiaro's case, the service entailed nothing short of being a personal miracle worker for guests, a grantor as well as a giver of special favors. As the Mark's chief favor broker, Finocchiaro went beyond the routine when it came to handling guest requests. Someone needed a prescription filled on an hour's notice on a Sunday? No problem. Giorgio knew the pharmacist— and he also had the druggist's home phone number.

And what made Finocchiaro particularly successful was that he performed his wizardry without an attitude. If a guest was too tired to go out to eat and wanted Chinese food delivered, he made sure the order was delivered promptly by the restaurant and paid for by the hotel, to be put on the bill later. And the food arrived with all the regular room service amenities.

A first-time guest at the Mark called Finocchiaro and explained that she hadn't been to New York in ten years and wanted to come back for only one purpose: to attend the Metropolitan Opera and go backstage to talk with soprano Jessye Norman. Giorgio got her the best seats in the house and then, through his contacts, finessed the meeting between star and fan.

Anyone who craved some great Italian food knew to go to Giorgio. Unlike most hotel concierges, he didn't just recommend a specific restaurant; he called the place and recommended *you* to them. That act of personal follow-through made all the difference in the world.

Before Finocchiaro came to the Mark, he had been properly seasoned at New York's Pierre Hotel for six years. "If I've learned anything," he says, "it's that no request is too bizarre, and that for service to be truly great it has to be subtle and understated. Ego cannot get in the way. I'm not a hero," he maintains, "but I know how to make someone else a hero."

In many cases, the concierge is the *only* person who can get the job done. The problem, however, is that most hotels use the word *concierge* but few use the actual person. The last place to look for a real concierge is on a concierge floor. There's a big difference between the two, and regular guests recognize it right away. Concierge floors offer guests who register there special services and amenities such as express check-in, continental breakfast, buffet-style snacks, or evening bed turndown. The reality is that the true concierges are few and far between at contemporary hotels.

A concierge floor, though, is not exactly a bad idea. Many guests who have price-shopped and are aware of this bring their families to the concierge floor's buffet, figuring this will save them money on dinner. It's not unusual to overhear parents telling their children to fill up on appetizers since this will be their dinner!

Will you find a concierge at a Four Seasons or a Ritz-Carlton? Yes. At the Peninsula? Of course. Likewise at the

Mandarin. However, other than at such upscale, privately owned and managed hotels, it's getting harder and harder to find real concierges.

MAKING FRIENDS WITH THE CONCIERGE

If you do manage to find a hotel with a true concierge, it's in your best interest to establish a relationship with that person. The concierge can be a lifesaver in certain situations, and, other than requests for something illegal or immoral, the concierge never uses the word *never*.

Concierges do much more than just secure hard-to-get tickets. The range of their services can cover everything from chasing down last-minute emergency tuxedo studs or shoelaces to securing reservations at restaurants long since fully booked.

But perhaps the best service provided by concierges—at least for me—is when entire cities are logjammed. Mardi Gras in New Orleans, the Super Bowl, the Democratic and Republican National Conventions, meetings of the World Bank, the Daytona 500, and other such events—these are occasions when concierges really shine.

For example, let's say you want to go to the Super Bowl, and it's in San Diego. You need a hotel room from the Friday before the game until the Monday morning after the game. You also need two tickets. Here's what you do. About five months before the event, rather than calling the hotel to make a room reservation, you call the concierge and introduce yourself. Tell the concierge that you want to come to the Super Bowl, and that you want four rooms and eight tickets. Give the concierge your credit card number. You'll get your rooms reserved through the concierge.

But wait a minute. You needed only two tickets and one room. Why ask for eight tickets and four rooms? Because

CELEBRITY ALIASES: Here's something else concierges know: which celebrities are staying at your hotel. More often than not, stars and other public figures use aliases when they check in. Here are a few:

NAME	ALIAS
Sharon Stone	Phoebe Turner
John Travolta	J.T. Smith
Diana Ross	Miss Orange
Jim Carrey	Fettucine Alfredo, Pete Moss
Elton John	Bobo Latrine, Sir Humphrey Handbag, Sir Brian Bigbum, Sir Dixon Clit
Rod Stewart	Sid James
Phil Collins	Peter Brinks
Ringo Starr	Richard Monaco
Bono of U2	J.C. Penny
Ozzy Osbourne	Harry Bollocks, Prince Albert
Mick Jagger	David James
Jerry Hall	Mrs. Robinson
John Wayne Bobbitt	Les Johnson
Rosie O'Donnell	Mr. Fred Beasley
Brad Pitt and Jennifer Aniston	Mr. & Mrs. Ross Vegas
David Schwimmer	Rupert Pumpkin
Bruce Willis	Wee Willie Wonka
Snoop Doggy Dogg	Hannibal Lechter
Lauren Holly	Andy Pandy
Tiger Woods	B. Simpson
Kevin Costner	Frank Farmer
Jimmy Buffett	Mr. Keys, Ward Robe
Robert Duvall	Robert Pedraza
Tom Selleck	Jack Ramsey
Patrick Swayze	Mr. Bizarro
Lance Bass	Dr. Seuss's real name, Ted Geisel
Sean "Puffy" Combs	Tony Montana (Al Pacino character in *Scarface*)
Matt Damon	Dickie Greenleaf (Jude Law's character in *The Talented Mr. Ripley*)

you're about to participate in an investment that will not only make the concierge happy, but will ensure that your hotel stay and the two tickets you actually wanted are essentially free. This actually works, and constitutes a little-known concierge finesse.

At some point between the time you call the hotel and about three weeks before the big game, the concierge is going to call *you*. The concierge will diplomatically ask whether you really need all eight tickets and all four rooms. Of course you don't. So, using the concierge as the unofficial broker, you will release three rooms and sell six tickets at a huge profit. This will satisfy the concierge and make six other people very happy because they managed to get tickets. But you get to be the happiest of all, because the money you've made selling those six tickets that you didn't want in the first place is enough to pay for your hotel room and the two tickets you originally needed.

A similar tactic can be used for getting hotel rooms during peak times when it seems that all city hotels are booked solid. Let's say you need a hotel room so you can get to the Final Four college basketball championship. But all the hotels claim they are sold out or even oversold. Can you trust that claim? Not necessarily.

There's a big difference between a booked room and a *blocked* room. For major annual events like this, large groups of rooms are held, or blocked, by advertisers, television networks, large corporate sponsors, and the event organizing committees. Concierges are a terrific resource in this situation because they know who controls those blocks. Inevitably, people block more rooms than they eventually need. In many cases, these rooms have also been prepaid. Concierges can help because they are in a position to contact the parties who control the blocks to see whether they might want to release some of their rooms. The hotel can't release the room, but the block holder can—and often at an attractive price.

AT YOUR SERVICE

If money is no object, concierges rock because they are all about unusual hotel services—things that can't be found in guidebooks or brochures. They are also the enablers, the people who can really make things happen both outside of the hotel and, often, if you know how to ask, inside it as well.

In the intense and sometimes desperate attempt to compete and differentiate themselves from other properties, many hotels are offering unique, over-the-top, and sometimes rather strange hotel services. You won't necessarily find these listed in the brochures, and some are no more than gimmicky stunts. But a few are surprisingly useful and provide, at the very least, a very different hotel experience.

When I stayed at the Hilton in Wichita Falls, Texas, each morning I watched an employee run out to the front of the hotel and wash the windows of every car in the parking lot. At the Sheraton in Shanghai, a desk clerk motioned for me to follow him one night, and seconds later I found myself in a hidden bowling alley inside the hotel.

Then there was the time I asked for change at the St. Francis Hotel in San Francisco and noticed that all the coins were new and shiny. Actually, they were just shiny. For years, the hotel had run the world's only hotel money laundry. It turned out that "clean money" had been a St. Francis trademark since 1938, when the hotel introduced the service for guests who didn't want their white gloves soiled by dirty silver dollars. Arnold Batliner could be found in a back room of the hotel, polishing coins. "It's of diminishing value," said one hotel official at the time, "and most of our guests don't even know about it. But we will continue it as long as Arnold's here."

Well, Arnold died a few years ago, so don't expect mint-condition coins the next time you're at the St. Francis. But many other unusual hotel services remain.

If you are a stargazer, the Hyatt Regency Maui offers guests a special rooftop astronomy program from its Lahaina Tower. And if you're ever visiting the Taj Mahal Hotel in Mumbai or the Taj Palace Hotel in Delhi, you can seek the advice of their twenty-four-hour resident astrologers.

For those who desire the utmost in discretion, the Mandarin Hotel in Hong Kong offers blind masseurs, who are on call twenty-four hours a day. (A similar service is provided at the Chosun hotel in Seoul, Korea.) Now what is the demand for a blind masseur? They are often used by public officials and celebrities—people who don't really want to be seen by anyone. They are also used by guests who are simply too timid to be seen in the nude.

As you might expect, many hotels have unusual services that focus on cuisine. Especially in the Pacific Northwest, a number of hotels allow guests to bring their freshly caught fish or fowl to the executive chef, who will then prepare it at dinner. (Remember, all you have to do is ask.)

Perhaps the nicest part of waking up at Las Brisas, in Acapulco, Mexico, is opening the "magic box" in your casita. Early each morning, attendants quietly visit each of the hotel's three hundred casitas and open the outside door to the box. Trays containing baskets of fruit, a thermos of hot coffee, and fresh-baked sweet rolls and croissants are inserted. Another nice touch at Las Brisas is that each casita has its own swimming pool, and once each day another attendant quietly appears and places dozens of fresh, bright red hibiscus flowers in the pool.

Having a tough time sleeping? The Hotel Burnham in Chicago features a pillow library stocked with an assortment of shapes and fillings, including a five-foot-long body pillow. I've tried these body pillows, and I'll let you assume anything you want, but I must warn you: you end up liking the pillow so much you're tempted to, uh, name it!

If by chance you insist on traveling with your own horse, a

number of local hotels in Melbourne, Australia, provide special equine accommodations. (Outmoded Australian innkeeper's laws require hoteliers to provide shelter and care for horses.) Thus, these hotels maintain suitable stabling and fodder on a daily basis. At this writing, no horses have yet checked in.

Some other unique hotel services that are available through the concierge include these:

- The Ritz-Carlton firewood concierge in Boston offers, free of charge, a choice of four types of firewood for your room. The menu includes birch (strong heat, burns fast), cherry (fragrant, burns slowly), oak (a light scent), and maple (sweet-smelling).

- The Ritz-Carlton in Philadelphia has a hot chocolate sommelier who will pour you everything from a "liquid s'more" to alcohol-spiked renditions of the much-loved beverage.

- The Ritz-Carlton in Hong Kong offers a wide variety of butler-drawn baths on its new bath menu. They include the Chinese Herbal Bath, featuring balancing and calming agents; the Gentleman's Bath, spiced with woody and earthy scents and accompanied by a fine cigar, a glass of cognac, and a plate of lobster canapés; the Ladies Bath, scented with geranium and melissa essences, accompanied by a healthy and refreshing glass of freshly squeezed carrot juice, watermelon, and a selection of crudités.

- Guests at the Portman Ritz-Carlton in Shanghai are invited on a one-of-a-kind city tour—on the general manager's motorcycle. DeCocini reveals his favorite city spots from a vantage point few tourists will ever experience: in a sidecar next to his limited-edition Chang Jiang 750cc motorcycle.

- San Francisco's Mandarin Oriental offers new guests Welcome Tea. During check-in, the front desk clerk calls a room service attendant, who, once you've arrived at your room, quickly brings up a pot of refreshing jasmine tea.

- The Las Ventanas al Paraiso in Los Cabos, Mexico, provides telescopes in all sixty-one rooms. Each room has a patio, and guests receive updated maps of the stars. Every Tuesday and Friday night, the resort offers stargazing evenings on the beach.

- The Regency Hotel in New York City offers a service called the Tuck-In Butler. The Tuck-In Butler, named Pinto, will come to your room and tuck your child into bed with milk and cookies and a bedtime story. He also has such emergency items as balloons and nightlights for weepy children who are reluctant to go to bed.

- The Rancho Bernardo Inn in San Diego, California, lets diners e-mail or fax what they want for dinner seventy-two hours ahead to its El Bizcocho restaurant.

- Each room in the Opus Hotel in Vancouver is equipped with a handheld oxygen dispenser. Benefits cited include increased metabolism, energy, and exercise performance, and the ability to neutralize toxins. This is helpful if you have a hangover.

- The 237-room W Hotel in Mexico City's funky Polanco neighborhood (the first W Hotel in Latin America) has hammocks in the showers for those who find the prospect of standing too tiresome.

- The Kerry Centre Hotel in Beijing has an in-line skating track and a regulation NBA basketball court. And in Chicago, at the House of Blues hotel, you can go bowling.

- The Marquis Fitness Center at the JW Marriott in Seoul includes a scuba pool, where guests can get their Professional Association of Diving Instructors (PADI) certification.

- The Houstonian Hotel in uptown Houston, the Venetian in Las Vegas, and the Fairmont in Chicago all offer guests the use of a rock-climbing wall.

- The Shangri-La Hotel in Singapore provides the thrill of rock climbing without the danger, thanks to a rock-climbing simulator that features adjustable speed and gradient controls.

- If you have a long layover in Tokyo, or are simply frustrated by waiting in airport lines, the Radisson Hotel Narita Airport will let you rappel down the side of the eleven-story hotel.

- The Hotel Bel Ami in Paris provides its guests with a menu of seven different mineral waters available at every minibar, including:

  Badoit—Originally prescribed by local doctors in the eighteenth century, the water of Saint Galmier in the Auvergne region of France has a small percentage of fluorine, which helps prevent tooth decay and assists the digestion process.

  Evian—This mineral-rich water has a neutral pH that helps eliminate sodium and is beneficial for kidney and digestive problems.

  Chataldon—This water is praised for its healing properties.

  Bru—This Belgian water was used during baptism.

  Thonon—This mineral water originates from natural springs.

  Perrier—This water is naturally carbonated and light in minerals.

Acqua Minerale Ferrarelle—This water is originally from Italy and has thermal proprieties.

- Hotel Teatro in Denver has taken relaxation to a new level with an innovative nighttime service: an Aveda Muscle Restoration Bath, served with a tubside tumbler of scotch and a bottle of water.

- At the Ramada Grand Hotel in Budapest, guests receive complimentary dental examinations.

- The Sonesta Hotel in Key Biscayne offers the world's first Relay Store and Segway Excursion Center, so now guests can rent the unique scooters, starting at $25 per hour.

- At Le Grand Hotel du Cap-Ferrat on the Côte d'Azur in France, a man named Pierre Grunberg (no relation to this author) spends every day at the hotel's magnificent pool teaching guests how to swim. He uses a salad bowl to help with breathing techniques in the water. He's taught everyone from Pablo Picasso to heads of state, as well as their children. You won't find him in the brochure—just ask for Pierre.

- At the Benjamin Hotel in New York, you have your choice (if you know to ask) among feather, buckwheat, or water-filled pillows.

- For travelers who find it hard to squeeze in regular exercise, Hilton Hotels Corporation is providing the option for guests to request a treadmill in their rooms. Under the "Get Fit with Hilton" program, guests can request an in-room treadmill for $15 a day.

- The champagne bar at the Hotel Villa Magna in Madrid offers a choice of more than one hundred French champagnes.

- Guests get an extra set of keys when they check in at the Ramada Hotel O'Hare, Chicago. The hotel's $88-per-day rate includes a compact car with unlimited mileage.

- The Palace Hotel in Beijing has solved its guests' irritation at having to remove the dust from their shoes, a problem that intensifies with the amount of coal burned locally during the winter months. A gleaming shoeshine stand from Istanbul can now be found in the lobby, manned by Francis, in full Chinese costume. And to pamper Japanese guests, the Palace barbershop now caters to Japanese clients. Toshide Ishibashi administers the traditional head and shoulder massage before beginning the hairstyle or treatment.

- The Hostellerie Lenoir in the Ardennes area of France, has a custom of serving dining guests with flowers in the same colors as their cars.

CHAPTER 9

Land of the Fee, Phone of the Brave

A friend of mine who owns about forty hotels relates the following story. It's the middle of winter. A man in Chicago is sick and tired of the cold weather, the sleet and the snow, and the general bleakness of a Midwest winter. He wants to get away to a resort in the sun and play some golf.

Impulsively, he hops on the first plane heading south, to Florida. Upon arrival, he instructs a cab driver to take him to a great golf resort. A few minutes later, he's there. He asks the cab driver to wait. He runs up to the front desk and asks if they have a room. Yes, but it's $800 a night. Too rich for his blood. He's on a budget. So he hops back in the cab and heads for a second location. But the room there is also steep: $700 a night. He tries six more resorts, all priced about the same. And finally, as he's about to give up, the cab driver takes him to a beautiful resort on the water. When he asks the room rate, he's pleasantly astonished: just $300 a night.

Fantastic, he thinks. He pays the cab driver and registers. He then asks the front desk clerk what the greens fees are. "Those are included in the price of your room, sir." Wow. How about golf clubs? Also included. The golf cart? Ditto.

When he checks into his room, he finds a beautiful golf shirt on the bed with a note from the general manager welcoming him to the hotel. On the nightstand sits a bottle of champagne on ice.

He puts on his new, complimentary golf shirt, drinks some of the champagne, and heads down to the golf course. He picks up his golf clubs, gets into the cart, and then realizes he's forgotten something.

He walks back to the pro shop. "I think I'm all set," he says. "But I just need some golf balls."

"No problem," says the clerk. "That will be $800."

"Eight hundred dollars for golf balls?" he asks, in shock.

"Yes," comes the nonplussed response.

"But how can that be?"

"Well, sir, at some hotels, they get you by the rooms . . ."

In hotel parlance, this is called *revenue enhancement.* Many hotels think they've been given a license to bill. But hotels rarely disclose these charges. And even when they are disclosed, they constitute the Nickel and Diming Hall of Shame. When booking a hotel room, you can never rely on the published room rate alone.

TAXATION WITHOUT DISCLOSURE

For starters, anytime a hotel can hide behind a municipal tax or public utility as a chance to add surcharges, it does. And more often than not, it does not reveal these taxes or charges when quoting its room rates. The next time you go to pay your hotel bill, be prepared to face the fact that you just helped a city or state (and chances are, it's not one in which you live or vote) to build a new sports complex or convention center or decrease a huge budget deficit.

Essentially, this constitutes taxation without representation. And those taxes can be huge. If you're a business traveler on a per diem or just a leisure traveler on a budget, you've just busted it.

Whenever you are booking a room, you need to ask the questions. Do not expect the hotel to volunteer the tax rates or the amounts. And they can be considerable.

Hotels should be up in arms over this. One study, done more than ten years ago, showed that, on average, the number of rooms rented at a hotel declines about 4.4 percent for every 10 percent increase in taxes. You pay the tax. The hotel rents fewer rooms. It's a lose-lose situation.

And it's not just big cities doing the taxing. The Wilmington, North Carolina, city council approved a 3 percent room tax increase to build a new downtown convention center. In Davis County, Utah, a bed tax was renewed to build an $11 million conference center. And in the height of irony, lawmakers in Orange, Texas, were considering raising the bed tax from 4 to 7 percent so that they'd have enough money to promote tourism!

In the hotels' defense, these local and state taxes are additional charges that they cannot control. By law, they must charge them. Still, hotels do a terrible job of full disclosure about taxes when quoting room rates. Why? On the surface—but *only* on the surface—they want to be competitive on official rate.

Recently, I called ten hotels across the country, ranging from the Peninsula in New York City to a Holiday Inn in California. I asked each hotel what its best room rate was for that evening. In ten out of ten cases, not one hotel mentioned the taxes when quoting the rate.

But what about the charges and fees the hotels *can* control? This is an area where hotels fail miserably across the board.

THE SURCHARGE EXPRESS

"Right now, just about every hotel is looking for ways to increase revenue," says Bjorn Hanson, PricewaterhouseCoopers's major hospitality consultant, "so they're throwing out whatever they think they can get away with. They're essentially gauging guest resistance. Over time, the major chains are hoping these charges can be quietly institutionalized."

Hanson is clearly not happy about these charges, since he travels nearly a hundred thousand miles a year, which means he is staying in a lot of hotels. Not long ago, he was traveling to the Arizona Biltmore. As a test, he had his secretary call and ask whether there would be any additional charges. No, she was assured. However, when Hanson checked out he found a $12 housekeeping surcharge on his bill. He complained to the front desk clerk. The clerk refused to take it off his bill. He complained to the general manager, who said it would be taken off.

A few days later, the charge showed up on his credit card bill. And only after he disputed that was the charge finally removed. "The absurd thing about this is that if you add the time I spent and my secretary spent on this against my normal hourly consultancy fees (ironically, often charged to hotels), on a time/value basis this was an outrageous waste of time. But I did it based on principle," he commented.

It goes from bad to worse. For example, some early-departure fees now average $50. This is truly absurd. If the city is full, then the hotel could easily re-rent the room in the event you check out early. If the city was empty to begin with, the hotel should be happy you stayed there for as long as you did.

Extra fees can be built into all kinds of small services. Some hotels charge up to $5—that's right, $5—per page to send faxes, and some add handling charges of up to $7 for receiving FedEx packages.

Believe it or not, some hotels in New England have assessed "processing" fees for canceled reservations, even when the reservations were canceled way in advance. To add insult to injury, a number of hotels have changed the rules about cancellation. For years, you could cancel your reservation without penalty up until 6 P.M. on the day you were checking in. Now, many hotels are enforcing a rule that penalty-free cancellations must be completed at least forty-eight hours prior to check-in. Often, guests are not notified of this policy.

Then there are energy surcharges. A number of large hotel chains—Hilton, Wyndham, and others—levied these surcharges during the power crunch of 2002, even in cities where the power companies or states didn't impose them! It didn't take long for some hotel guests—in other words, lawyers—to figure that out. Wyndham International settled a nationwide class action lawsuit over the energy surcharges. What did the plaintiffs receive in the settlement? A coupon for a $15 discount for their next stay at a Wyndham hotel. The settlement amount and terms notwithstanding, the message sent by the lawsuit was clear: if you want to charge us extra for something, you have to make your case.

These days, a large assortment of new, restructured, renamed, or unjustified charges are suddenly finding their way onto your hotel bill.

In a desperate effort to increase revenue, many hotels and resorts have, well, resorted to a squeeze play—and, in fact, they call it a *resort* fee. I call it nothing less than a "fee for all." The presumption, of course, has always been that when we stay in a hotel and pay the room rate, we're paying for basic services. But maybe not.

One hotel in Key West hits guests with an $11 "convenience" fee, which raises the question: convenient for whom? And what does that fee supposedly cover? Ice, beach towels, beach chairs, and daily room cleaning. That's on top of the hotel's regular room rate of $259 a night—so, what does *that* rate cover?

Some resorts charge a daily $27 resort fee and claim it's to cover tips to bellstaff and housekeepers. Ask the bellstaff and the housekeepers at those resorts whether they ever see any of that money. Furthermore, none of those folks refuse tips in protest that they've already been paid. Some resorts seem to be charging even for the swimming pool—and this is not just in the United States but in Europe as well. Recently, the Savoy group in the United Kingdom added a 5 percent discretionary service charge to bills at its London properties.

Every once in a while, a hotel or resort can make an effective argument that the resort fee is good for both the hotel and the guest. At the Homestead in Hot Springs, Virginia, a 15 percent service fee is added. But it includes dining room gratuities, valet parking, afternoon tea, admission to the fitness center and indoor pool, two movies nightly, local calls, free 800-number access, and transportation to and from the golf course and equestrian center. Sounds like a great deal—and I suppose if you're making calls on the golf course from your horse while parking your car on the way to afternoon tea before you do a mini movie marathon, it makes sense. But what if you're just staying at the hotel and renting a room? That 15 percent charge seems usurious.

The real problem with resort fees, however, is in the area of full disclosure. A number of lawsuits were successfully filed against hotels and resorts for not revealing the fee at either the time the reservation was made or when the hotel guest checked in.

As a traveler, you have a responsibility to ask—either when making a reservation or when checking in—whether a resort fee will be charged. And keep in mind that many hotels now make that fee optional—which means it is essentially negotiable as well.

THE UNSAFE HOTEL SAFE

Hotels spend about $140 each to buy and install basic electronic in-room safes. As I've said before, what does an in-room safe say? Number one, we don't trust our security. Number two, we don't trust our staff. And, oh yes, we're charging you upward of $3 per day to use the safe! To make matters worse, under every state's innkeeper's law, the hotel is not liable for anything taken from an in-room safe; it is liable only for items missing from the safe-deposit boxes near the check-in counter or at the front desk.

Assuming that the hotel is only fully occupied for half the

year and that only half the guests use the safe, the hotel handily recoups its investment. My advice is to use the safe-deposit boxes downstairs, with one exception: some safe manufacturers are now guaranteeing up to $5,000 for any loss from an in-room safe due to forced entry. Ironically, that's actually a higher limit of liability than hotels offer for their safe-deposit boxes. One caveat to this is the phrase "forced entry." At some hotels, there are too many master keys floating around—no forced entry, no liability.

THE DARTH VADER MINIBAR

I have a love-hate relationship with hotel minibars. Almost every time I stay at a hotel, I enter into a staring contest with that minibar, and I always seem to blink first. I open that door and—ka-ching!—the charges mount up.

I first discovered the real perils of the minibar about fourteen years ago. I was in London to attend my cousin Sean's wedding. I was arriving late to the hotel, so I told some of my friends to go up to my room ahead of me. My youngest cousin, Jess, still in college, knew all about dormitory rooms—but not about hotel rooms. He entered my room about an hour before I got there, spotted the minibar, and exclaimed, "Wow—free food!" In less than sixty minutes, the human vacuum cleaner consumed everything nonalcoholic in that bar. And I received a bill for £185—or about $277! From that point on, Jess has been known in my family as "Mr. Minibar."

Today, minibars still abound—and they're worse than ever. The latest "Darth Vader" models are based on infrared technology and are posted with warnings that if you open the door to the minibar and do anything more than just look at the items inside, you will be billed. Anything you touch is debited on your account. With an automatic minibar, you have only fifteen seconds to make your decision after picking up an item. If you don't put it right back, you are charged for it. The technology is very accurate, but it can be a nightmare at checkout. No matter that warning signs are posted all over the guest rooms, the ease with which the charges can mount still does not register with guests. A number of hotels now even charge a restocking fee to refill minibars, which may be as much as 20 percent of the total cost of the items consumed.

In my first Travel Detective book, I recommended that you buy what you want at a supermarket or convenience store on the way into the hotel, and then ask the bellhop or housekeeping to empty the minibar. I stand by this recommendation. Wyndham CEO Fred Kleisner believes that nothing in the minibar should cost anything more than what's in the vending machine down the hall. "I just don't think you should have to pay $15 for a can of peanuts," Kleisner complains. This makes sense, but only if the hotels that bear the Wyndham name play along—and not all of them do.

One hotel in Los Angeles, the Wyndham Checkers, apparently didn't get the memo. When *New York Times* columnist Joe Sharkey stayed there, he couldn't help but notice the prices. "Business travelers hate paying felony-hijack-level prices for a bag of crackers," he wrote.

Indeed, the minibar prices that Sharkey found at Checkers were outrageous. A 1.5-ounce bag of pretzels was $3; a pack of chewing gum and a regular roll of Life Savers cost $3.50.

Not long after Sharkey made his minibar pricing discovery and wrote about it, the Wyndham name came off the property. The place then became a Hilton. Today, it's Wyndham policy that minibar prices must match local vending machine prices. Period. Sadly, I don't know of other large chains that have instituted this policy.

WATER, WATER EVERYWHERE

As if the minibar isn't bad enough, along comes something worse, the item that many hotels place *on top* of that minibar: the very welcome, but extremely expensive, bottle of water.

How about $6 for a five-hundred-milliliter bottle of natural spring water? On a per-unit basis, this is probably the highest markup in a hotel. Hotels buy their bottled water from large distributors (such as Coca-Cola, which sells the Dasani brand) for about $9 for a case of thirty-two bottles. That works out to a cost for the hotels of just slightly more than 28¢ per bottle, which is a markup—if you're careless enough to consume that water—of more than 5,700 percent!

Six dollars for a bottle of water? Nine dollars for a candy bar? The only thing a hotel stands to gain by charging such exorbitant minibar prices is an alienated guest who will not return. I keep telling hoteliers that whether someone has a great stay at your hotel or a lousy stay, the only thing they're going to remember is that ridiculously expensive bottle of water.

Another problem associated with those bottles of water is that a number of guests, angry at the high cost, will open the bottles, drink them, and then refill them with tap water out of the bathroom faucet, then replace the bottle on top of the minibar, hoping that no one will notice. Just one more reason not to drink those bottles!

But it gets worse. Some guests open beer cans by punching a hole in the bottom of the can, emptying the beer into a glass, and replacing the can into the minibar. Other guests actually devour chocolate bars from the middle. They very carefully push the little bars out of the wrappers, unfolding the foil, and eating only the middle pieces. The two ends are then placed back into the foil.

And when it comes to alcohol, the big abuse happens with scotch. Some ingenious guests open the little bottles of whiskey, then replace the alcohol with tea.

This might explain the growth in the number of Darth Vader minibars!

TAKEN TO THE CLEANERS

Hotel laundry is another huge-markup item, but many guests feel they have no choice but to use the laundry services offered by the hotels.

Merv Griffin once told me a wild—but true—story. Griffin, who in addition to being an entertainer is also a hotelier (he owns the Beverly Hilton Hotel, for starters), was staying at a luxury hotel in Paris. He wanted to send two shirts out to be laundered. But when he filled out his laundry slip, he noticed how much the hotel wanted to charge him for each shirt. "On principle alone," he said, "I couldn't do it." Then he looked across the street and spied the solution. There was a thrift shop about a half a block away. Griffin, who swears this is true, took the shirts downstairs, walked the short distance to the thrift shop, and "donated" his shirts. The next afternoon, he returned to the thrift shop and bought the shirts back for $2 each. Of course, the thrift shop had laundered the shirts the night before!

I'm not recommending such an extreme solution. But the fact remains that hotel laundries are large profit centers, even though hotels usually don't have a laundry on the premises, and even fewer have a dry cleaning operation. They have to send your clothes out.

So here are two solutions that the valet won't tell you about. It's often cheaper to tip the bellhop $5 to take your clothes to the neighborhood laundry or dry cleaner. This is a practical solution both in the United States and especially overseas.

However, if that's not feasible, do what I do. (This works exceptionally well in the United States.) It is often far less expensive for my office to FedEx to my hotel a supply of clean shirts, underwear, socks, and suits than it is for me to send them out. I then FedEx the clothes back to my office to be laundered. The only additional expense, if any, is for the hotel to press my suit.

THE BIG PHONE HANGUP

My favorite area in which hotels nickel-and-dime guests is phone and Internet charges.

Hotels argue that their phone systems are a huge capital expense, and they have to do everything they can to recover that investment. But isn't the cost of installing the hotel phone system already figured into amortizing the hotel's debt—and used to calculate the initial room rate? Of course it is, as is the cost of double-glazing your room windows or installing the hotel elevators. (And let's not forget that marble in the lobby and the chandelier in the ballroom.)

Nevertheless, hotels continue to try to make their case for charging exorbitant rates for guests who make calls from hotel phones. One general manager at a Holiday Inn insisted that his phone costs outpaced his profits. To prove that point, he claimed that his hotel is charged a maintenance fee of between $35 and $45 per month for each phone line. He has fifty-two phones installed at his property and, assuming a worst-case scenario, that means his monthly maintenance costs are $2,340.

But some basic arithmetic reveals his true costs. Assuming that only half his rooms are occupied at any one time, he needs to earn only $1.56 per phone line per day to cover his expenses—and he's taking in far more than that. That certainly discounts the argument that phones are a loss leader.

These days, hotels are required to fully disclose their phone charges in an accessible place in your room. Most put their rate cards near the phones, but this doesn't mean they're necessarily easy to read or understand.

At least one San Francisco hotel informed guests on its disclosure card that the only free call they would get in the hotel was if they called another guest room. I presume the management thought it was being cute when it did this, but the resulting joke was that many guests read the card and *did* call other guest rooms—to discuss the rate card!

At the Walt Disney World Swan and Dolphin hotels in Florida, the first sixty minutes of each local call are free. It appears that all 800 numbers are also free. But not really. The fine print at the bottom of the rate disclosure card reveals that the hotel has bundled 800-number, credit card, and third-party billed calls into that dreaded daily $8 "resort" fee.

At the Essex House in New York, local calls are billed at $1.50 for the first five minutes, and then 15¢ a minute after that. But an 800 number is billed at $2, plus 10¢ a minute after the first hour. That works out to $6 an hour for a supposedly toll-free number. Not surprisingly, thousands of hotel guests who travel with their laptop computers—myself included—have been stunned to discover that they've racked up a huge phone bill by the end of their hotel stay. Why? Because they logged on to the Internet and forgot to disconnect.

Dialing a direct long-distance call from the Essex House? Call the paramedics. You will pay operator-assisted day rates, plus a $4 hotel surcharge, plus 125 percent of the cost of the call as an additional charge. Dialing within New York state? Again, you'll be hit with operator-assisted day rates, plus a $2.82 hotel surcharge, plus an additional charge of 238 percent. AT&T is the service provider listed on the card.

AT&T was one of the exhibitors at a recent convention for hotel owners and operators. I visited their booth. Guess what they were charging hotels for service: for long-distance interstate calls, just $0.022 per minute! This means that the markup for just a single five-minute local call at the Essex House is astronomical: it costs you $1.50. The same phone call costs the hotel only *11¢*. A five-minute long-distance call at the Essex House will cost you $2 in operator-assisted day rates (at 40¢ per minute), plus a $4 surcharge, plus a 125 percent additional charge, for a total of $13.50, not including tax. The cost to the hotel is *still just 11¢!*

The situation is worse overseas. Not long ago, I was staying at a hotel in London. Its phone rate card stated that there were no access charges to use MCI, Sprint, or AT&T phone cards. That seemed quite reasonable. So I called the toll-free number for my MCI card, and a U.S. operator answered. "This is your U.S. operator," she said. This struck me as strange, since most of my MCI calls normally go through without operator assistance. I asked whether she worked with MCI. "I'm your U.S. operator" was all she would say.

I did some digging to uncover the scam. The hotel was trying to avoid complaints from its guests for wildly inflated phone charges, but it still wanted the extra revenue. So it contracted with a private phone company in Philadelphia, programming its phone system at the hotel to automatically route all 800 calls to AT&T, Sprint, and MCI directly to that company. Unsuspecting guests thought they were simply making a call through their own phone service operator. No long-distance phone charges showed up on their hotel bills. It was only after they returned home and received their long-distance phone bills that the shock hit them. That three-minute London–to–Los Angeles call, which should have cost about $5 on their MCI bill, came to more than $19—$5 went to MCI, and the hotel and the company in Philadelphia split the difference. This tactic is called alternate operator service (AOS), and you need to be aware of it—and avoid it—at all costs.

It is no wonder that at some foreign hotels, revenue from phone services has sometimes amounted to nearly 9 percent of the company's cash flow. However, revenue from phone services at U.S. hotels has dropped to about 1 percent of cash flow. Why?

Because many hotel guests have simply revolted and are using their cell phones to make all their calls. This is feasible as long as you can get a clear signal in your hotel room or in some other convenient location in the city in which you are staying.

One recent survey showed that on a typical hotel stay, even those of us who claim to use only our cell phones end up using the hotel phone for our computers or to access our own long-distance services about four times a day. Thus, on a three-night stay, we've paid an outrageous $24, at $2 per call, just to use so-called toll-free numbers! In a three-hundred-room hotel, assuming the hotel is only 50 percent occupied, that's an additional $8,400 per week in pure profit.

Confronted with dwindling profits, a number of hotels have decided to bundle phone charges and offer this package as a "discount" service. Recently, I checked into the Westin Peachtree in Atlanta, and found tent cards at the registration counters offering a flat $16 rate for twenty-four hours of unlimited local, toll-free, and domestic long-distance calls. Based on what the hotel would normally charge, it was a great deal. But even at $16, it was also a great deal for the hotel. Based on that $.022 per minute that the phone companies charge the hotels, I would need to be on the phone for thirteen straight hours before the hotel lost money on the deal. Very few of us spend more than eight hours a day in a hotel room to begin with.

What many guests do not know is that, just like any other charge, these phone charges are negotiable at hotels. Some hotels offer similar bundled deals for between $8 and $12 a day, but still other hotels are willing to negotiate downward in order to keep your business. A friend of mine first haggles with the hotel, talking them down to the lowest possible room rate. As the clincher, he offers to confirm the deal and make the reservation if the hotel agrees to waive local and toll-free phone charges. Once any particular hotel makes that deal, he's set a precedent there.

If the hotel doesn't want to play, no problem. My friend simply calls a competitor and negotiates with them. It's important to note that this friend is not a meetings and convention planner. He doesn't control large blocks of hotel rooms. He's a solo business traveler who merely figured out how to play the game.

If you prefer not to negotiate, a stopgap measure is to use prepaid phone calling cards. They're not an ideal solution, but at least they're less expensive than paying hotel phone rates. AT&T offers the One Rate Card calling plan, which costs $1 a month with 25¢-a-minute charges and no connection fee. MCI offers a similar plan, for $2 a month with only 15¢-per-minute charges.

However, at least one hotel chain has come to grips with the phone charges it assesses guests, and has simply eliminated them. The Wyndham hotel chain was not alone in seeing its phone revenues evaporate. Like almost every other hotel, it also heard nothing but complaints from its most frequent guests about those phone charges. So the chain did some internal accounting and decided to roll the dice in a big way. The hotel management announced a great deal: guests who registered for its Wyndham by Request frequent-stay program, which cost nothing, could make toll-free calls with no additional charges whenever they stayed at a Wyndham hotel in North America. Their local calls would also be free. The coup de grâce was that all domestic long-distance calls would likewise be free. No bundling here—free.

Other hotel companies called Wyndham's move suicidal, a profit killer. How could a hotel chain afford to give its services away? Were the folks at Wyndham crazy? Not in the least. Their announcement hit a home run with frustrated travelers. Millions of dollars in market share suddenly switched to Wyndham. And the hotel's worst-case scenario never materialized: that hordes of hotel guests, sequestered inside their rooms, would call everyone they ever met.

As for the numbers, in its first year the program cost Wyndham just $68,000 in real-dollar phone charges. From the start, the program has been an overwhelming success. Travelers had been so upset for so long over outrageous hotel phone charges that when Wyndham announced its new phone deal, people flocked to register for the Wyndham frequent-stay program, not necessarily because they planned to make an excessive number of phone calls from their guest rooms, but simply because they liked the idea that they could if they wanted to.

Perhaps one of the best outcomes from the Wyndham deal is that travelers now have an additional negotiating tool when making hotel reservations. Wyndham's program has made other hotels' negotiating positions that much weaker—and yours that much stronger—when you are trying to minimize or even eliminate the draconian hotel phone charges.

THE INTERNET CONNECTION

Although some of the phone battles have been won, hotels have found another means to raise in-room revenue, in the form of high-speed Internet access. A number of hotels price this service at up to $12 per night for a fast logon. But lately, most savvy hotel guests aren't taking the bait.

The smarter hotels that don't nickel-and-dime their guests when it comes to technology are the ones that profit. Consider the case of Wingate Inns. They were the first chain to offer free high-speed Internet access to their guests and see their occupancy rate increase.

The numbers tell the story. A one-hundred-room Wingate hotel charging for high-speed or broadband connections might hope to make an additional $270 per month. But Wingate discovered that the same hotel could earn an additional $8,000 per month in higher occupancy rates if it offered the service for free. About 30 percent of Wingate guests use the in-room Internet access, versus only 4 percent of the guests at hotels that charge for it.

Some hotels are getting the message. Comfort Suites, Hilton Garden Inn, and Courtyard by Marriott are three brands that say they are moving toward free access.

LET US ENTERTAIN YOU

Ironically, the one hotel room profit center about which guests hardly ever complain is in-room entertainment, otherwise known as movies. These are movies on demand. Lodgenet, for example, currently provides entertainment services to more than 5,700 hotels representing 950,000 guest rooms. Very soon, more than 55 percent of all hotel rooms will receive digital services. In-room revenues have jumped 37 percent as a result. Second only to the minibar, the in-room movie boasts the highest markup because there is no labor involved.

Some hotels are trying to bundle the movie service into the room cost. One general manager told me he offers a special deal at his hotel that includes the room, a movie, and breakfast. It was sort of a B&B idea, he told me. But as he looked at the numbers, he laughed. "We might have simply called it a P&B, a porn and breakfast deal. Just about everyone was watching the porn flicks. The movie was actually driving the room deal."

The best-selling type of movie in hotel rooms is porn films, by an overwhelming margin. In fact, adult movies generate 60 percent of total in-room entertainment revenue. Some hotels— for example, certain Ramada Inns—offer a package for diehard guests: $21.99 for unlimited viewing until noon. Although hotels keep an internal record of which movie you've watched, they wisely don't list them by title or type on your bill.

There's a growing interest in in-room music services. One

system tested sixty-five rooms at the Hilton Arlington and Towers in Virginia. When the hotel didn't charge for the music service, 35 percent of the guests listened to selections an average of two hours per day. But get ready: hotels are beginning to charge $4 to $5 a day for unlimited music and audio service. My prediction is that we won't pay. Many of us now travel with our own portable CD players and state-of-the-art digital MP3 players like Apple's iPod.

CHAPTER 10

What Hotel Room Service Won't Tell You

It was 2:30 on a slow, midweek afternoon in Maui. I was staying at the Hyatt Regency, a luxury resort hotel. I was hungry.

I found the room service menu and called. After ten rings, a tired voice answered and asked me to hold. I held for five minutes. Then I was disconnected.

When I called back, another voice answered and asked me to hold. I refused and promptly ordered a simple cheeseburger and a bottle of ginger ale. I gave the room service folks my name and room number and politely asked when I might be receiving the food.

"I really don't know," he said. "Could be thirty minutes. Could be an hour." He was wrong. An hour and twenty minutes later, a very soggy cheeseburger arrived.

Unfortunately, the Hyatt in Maui has no monopoly on bad room service. Throughout the world, there are dozens of hotels that compete for the honor of worst room service.

In fact, in certain countries, bad room service is expected. In China, hotels don't really understand the concept of room service. One Beijing hotel's room service menu offers "old snacks." There's often a language problem. Shanghai's Jing Jiang Hotel once offered "Mesals, smacks and Drinks to be served at the appointed time."

More often than not, however, hotels in America look upon dining in your room as an afterthought favor to guests rather than as a distinct and special service. I remember the time I was at the Winston Plaza Hotel, in Winston-Salem, North Carolina. It was eleven o'clock at night, and I hadn't eaten. I called room service. There was no answer. I then called the front desk. "I'm sorry sir," said the clerk, "but people here go to bed early, so room service closes early, too." But what about the guests? Traditionally, the concept of room service is simply that: a service provided, usually at extra cost, for hotel guests.

Occasionally, the extra cost gets a little out of hand. The sandwich was listed on the room service menu at the Beverly Hills Hotel as corned beef with sauerkraut, Russian dressing, and cheese. When a guest ordered one from room service, he asked them to hold the cheese. The sandwich arrived with the bill, which read: "Sandwich $9.95. No cheese $3." Extra charges indeed!

Of course, at some hotels you'd be a fool to expect room service to be anything more than a vending machine at the end of the hall. Nevertheless, if a hotel advertises that it has room service, it should deliver it.

CAN ROOM SERVICE DELIVER?

My first experience at the Hotel Vier Jahreszeiten (Four Seasons) in Munich, considered one of the top hotels in Europe, was that room service was expensive and frequently late, and they couldn't manage to keep the food hot. Conversely, not every motel defines room service as processed cheese wrapped in cellophane. So there are some surprises. Still, major hotels that host large conventions and meetings have absolutely no excuse for not providing excellent room service.

Room service also varies widely—and wildly—among hotel chains. While my experiences at the Hyatt in Maui were hardly terrific, just the opposite occurs with regularity at the Park Hyatt in Chicago. It's a smaller hotel, and a great deal of attention is paid to keeping guests happy. Not only is the room service efficient, but the menu and presentation of the in-room cuisine matches those at many upscale restaurants.

One hotel franchise that has remained consistent in room service quality is the Peninsula group. Not long ago, I mistakenly pushed the wrong button in my room at the Peninsula Hotel in Hong Kong. Less than twenty seconds later, two men appeared at my door—one held a tray of tea and crackers and the other asked whether I wanted the kitchen to cook anything for me. I wasn't hungry, but I was so embarrassed that I ordered something anyway.

Unfortunately, the consistency of room service quality at hotels is often disappointing—the menu is limited, the service tends to be slower than you expect, you pay more for the food, and it's often not very good. Such service can be characterized as "drop and run": the waiter arrives, he pushes the trolley into your room, you sign the check, and he runs off. This isn't because the hotel food and beverage staff doesn't care enough to provide good room service. In many cases, they simply can't due to built-in physical and logistical obstacles such as the size of the hotel kitchen, the distance between that kitchen and your room, and whether there is a dedicated room service staff and a dedicated room service elevator. These last two considerations are especially important during peak times—and when it comes to room service, there is only one peak time: *early morning*. But the main issue with room service really gets down to one specific: what you order from that room service menu can often mean the difference between an acceptable meal and an outright disaster.

First, let's talk about distances. In big-city hotels, distances are considered vertically. How high up are you? How long does the elevator take to reach your floor? At some hotels, the staff blocks off one elevator in the early morning hours to do nothing but handle room service orders.

At resort hotels and just about any hotel in Las Vegas the problems are compounded because horizontal distance must be accounted for as well. After you have checked in, take note of how long it actually takes you to get to your room. If you need an air traffic controller to find your room, a similar challenge awaits the room service waiter. Consider that in the time it takes that waiter to reach your room, your meal has lost both taste *and* value.

TRAY BIEN

There are certain items you should never order from room service. Let's start with breakfast. You'll find eggs Benedict on virtually every hotel room service menu. Don't do it. In restaurant parlance, eggs just don't travel well—especially eggs covered in thick sauces. The same principle applies to omelets, unless you want to use them later as flotation devices in the hotel pool.

Strangely enough, I regard hotel breakfast room service the same way I regard airline food. I order only individual fruit rather than a fruit plate or just cold cereal. Short of not giving you milk, these are the two things a hotel can't mess up. I avoid the fruit plate because hotels preplate them and I prefer fresh fruit to fruit that's already been cut and plated and has been sitting in a refrigerator with the obligatory scoop of cottage cheese for who knows how long. And I keep it simple: I order a bowl of berries or grapes. At least half the times I order this I'm told that I can have the grapes or berries as part of the fruit plate but not separately—proof right there that the fruit has been preplated. I will persist, asking whether there are any grapes or berries in the hotel's kitchen refrigerator. If the answer is no, I then call the main dining room, order a bowl of grapes or berries, and ask them to deliver it via room service—and, miraculously, the fruit arrives! Dealing with room service may occasionally require such cunning.

Here are some other red flag items. If you must have bread, order croissants or a muffin but not toasted bagels or toast itself. Order cold cereal, not oatmeal. Opt for a club sandwich instead of a hot sandwich. Remember, anything you order toasted or heated won't be hot by the time it arrives at your room.

Stay away from anything fried, either as an appetizer or as a side dish. What started out crispy will arrive cold and soggy. Admit it: how many times have you ordered french fries with your meal and actually been satisfied?

If you order cold beverages, make absolutely sure you ask for ice in a bucket or separate glass. If you don't, the carbonated drinks will be flat by the time they get to you and that ice tea will arrive diluted. In fact, it's best to order beverages in a bottle or can (remember my Diet Coke test?).

If you want to order that club sandwich, ask for an extra ingredient to be added so you know it will have to be made from scratch. You can go ahead and order a caesar salad, but insist that the dressing be on the side. And if you want pasta and prefer thin pasta, then be sure to ask for sauce on the side and request extra sauce because pasta absorbs it. Better yet, ask for your pasta to be cooked "a la minute."

Some other no-nos include:

- Grilled fish—the internal temperature tends to cool quickly so it's better to order a salad with grilled salmon on top

- Very rare meat

- Risotto

- Frozen cocktails

- Milk shakes

- Draft beer—order individual bottles instead

- Poached eggs

- Odiferous foods (aged cheeses, raw onions, etc.)

Believe it or not, you can find some values from room service:

- Some hotels offer room service prix fixe lunches and dinners.

- Order a pot of coffee rather than a cup.

- Order an appetizer and an entrée but not dessert. People tend to overorder their room service food, and much of it is left uneaten.

- Ask about portion sizes—a cup of soup is often about the same quantity as a bowl, depending on the serviceware, but it's cheaper to order a cup.

- Order two appetizers instead of an entrée.

The following advice is for those who want to apply the advanced room service course. At better hotels, there's nothing wrong with asking room service to deliver your food course by course instead of all at the same time. If you want toast, ask them to bring a toaster to your room. Many hotels will do this. Some hotels will even toss your salad in your room for you. But if you don't ask, you won't get the service.

My final piece of advice regarding room service is to watch out for double-dipping. I mentioned this in the first Travel Detective book, and since then the problem has only gotten worse. Examine your room service receipt carefully. Many hotels put a surcharge on room service to begin with, and some others add a $2.50 or $3.50 delivery charge. But that's not all. They may arbitrarily add a 15 to 18 percent gratuity and sales tax, and then they give you a subtotal—that's right, a *subtotal.* And guess what appears on the bill below that? A blank spot marked *tip.* If you're not careful, you'll end up paying $35 for that cheeseburger and soft drink.

There are some other important things you should know before you order room service. Is room service available twenty-four hours a day? Before September 11, 2001, many hotels offered round-the-clock room service. Now, many have cut back the hours drastically, or, if they offer late-night room service at all, it's from an extremely limited prepared-in-advance menu.

Insist that the person taking your room service order inform you when your food will arrive. The order should arrive within thirty minutes. If the room service representative hedges on a time of arrival, then politely state that you will not accept the food order after a certain time.

Remember, the hotel is not doing you a favor by providing this service. You're paying for it. An expensive cup of coffee is worthless if it arrives cold and an hour late.

If you dislike the thought of room service or find nothing appealing on that particular menu, do what I do. Ask the hotel concierge which restaurant makes the best take-out Chinese or Thai food closest to the hotel and will deliver. Chances are excellent that the concierge will already have their menu. When the food is delivered to the hotel, the concierge puts the charge on your bill and sends the delivery to your room. This is less expensive than room service, and you get what you want.

Some hotel guests just hate eating alone so a few hotels have introduced a possible solution to this dilemma, called "the maitre d's table." Most guests who travel alone opt to stay in their rooms and order room service rather than sit alone in a large hotel restaurant. However, at some hotels lone diners are asked to join the maitre d's table. This group of solitary diners often results in an interesting gathering. Of course, your table-mates might turn out to be bores. If that happens, well, there's always room service.

DINNER AT THE HOTEL RESTAURANT

For years, most in-house hotel restaurants were a necessary evil. They weren't expected to make money. They weren't expected to be good. No one aspired to work there—or eat there. Hotels simply took it for granted that they had to have one. And if you were staying at the hotel for more than two nights, it was likely that you'd eat there at least once.

The restaurant was, quite literally, the last resort inside the resort. You went there when you were too tired to go anywhere else, and the odds were good that you would suffer for your choice. Service was generally poor, and the menu was limited in choice and quality. To add insult to injury, the prices were usually inflated.

Today, not only are the guests eating in hotel restaurants, but people in the surrounding community are going there to eat as well. One of the biggest changes in the perception of hotel food is that the restaurants are being built or renovated and promoted as separate entities from the hotels. Many are free-standing restaurants that are not physically located in the hotel. Such a restaurant has its own name, marquee, and entrance.

Nowadays hotels might pay as much attention to the aesthetics of their restaurants as they do to the food they serve. But aesthetics will only get you into a hotel restaurant the first time. It's the food that will entice you to go back.

It is true that people eat with their eyes as well as with their mouths. The process starts with what you read on a hotel restaurant's menu, but even more fundamentally with *how* you read that menu. Hence, the new science of menu engineering. There's a real psychology to what appears on your hotel restaurant menu and how and where it appears. You need to be aware of this, or you may find yourself ordering something you didn't really want at a price you really can't afford to pay.

Menu engineering focuses on the center section of the menu. That is where hotel restaurants put the items they want to sell you at the highest prices, because it is where your eyes naturally land when you open that menu. If the food item has a high profit margin, that's where you'll find it—right smack in the center of the menu.

That's also where hotel restaurants put their prestige pricing items. Research indicates that about 20 percent of us will order the most expensive item that way. And often the reason for that is ego—people are trying to impress other people. One hotel offered a chocolate cake for dessert with edible twenty-four-karat gold leaf. It cost the hotel only $3 per slice, but the menu price was $14—and the chef couldn't make enough to keep up with the demand.

Certain menu items occasionally turn out to be "dogs"—and often this has to do with how the dish is named. An Italian restaurant featured a dish called Pizza with Funghi (*funghi* means "mushroom" in Italian). No one bought it. When they changed the name to English, the dish suddenly began selling— and at a higher price.

You will also find one item on every hotel restaurant menu that the chef puts there as a "safety" meal—intended either for children or for seniors. Often this will be a pasta dish such as spaghetti with marinara sauce. At some hotels, I generally order from the children's menu. Not only is it less expensive, but the food is simple and good.

> **FISH STORY:** The flyer for a Polish hotel informs prospective visitors: "As for the trout served you at the hotel Monopol, you will be singing its praise to your grandchildren as you like on your deathbed."

Most restaurants utilize "off-point" pricing. At a restaurant that uses this tactic, it is highly unusual to find anything on the menu for say, an even $12. $11.95 will be the price listed because diners tend to read this as a discounted price.

In order to make money, hotels employ a mathematical model for analyzing the profit potential of each individual item on the restaurant menu. "There are star items, plowhorses, and dogs," says Tina Ruggiero, a registered dietician who often consults with hotels about menu engineering.

A "star" item is a dish that contributes a high amount of profit margin, which might be anything from loin of pork to steak. Then there are items that make only a small contribution to a restaurant's profit margin—such as that Italian funghi pizza or a chicken dish that features an unfamiliar sauce. One way to get such items to move is to adjust the toppings or presentation—adding a demi-glace or a foie gras topping to an existing dish can change the diner's perception of it and boost orders for it. Of course, the price must be adjusted accordingly, too. The plowhorse menu item is a dependable dish with a low profit margin. This includes such staples as the venerable cheeseburger and anything from the kids' menu. Finally, there are the dogs—menu items that just don't move. This category includes things like beef stew served during the summer months, which is a strategy inevitably doomed to failure.

Let the diner beware—read your menu carefully. You might want to think twice before ordering anything from the center of the menu or any dish whose menu listing is surrounded by an eye-catching border. If you are seeking the best value, a good rule of thumb is to look at the first and last items on the entrée menu.

Also, be on the alert for waitstaff trained in the art of the upsell. These servers will suggest an appetizer to go with your entrée or a particular brand or vintage of wine. Learn to resist them.

If you're really looking for value at a hotel restaurant, don't just scan the menu looking for dishes you like; rather, read the menu carefully for buried items that might be just as good or better, but will almost always be less expensive.

SECRETS OF THE HOTEL BAR

If you tend to regard a hotel as a backdrop for drama or comedy and are entertained by the notion of a hotel as containing a complete three-act play, you need look no farther than the hotel bar for your amusement.

BAR NONE: The sign in a Norwegian lounge reads: "Ladies are requested not to have children in the bar."

At the best hotels, the bartenders are the central intelligence agency personified. Their role goes way beyond that of simple mixologists. A hotel bartender often surpasses the concierge in terms of guidance, information, and discretion. However, as in every other division of the hotel, the bar is expected to make a profit as well. What you order, how you order, and when you order can often make the difference between a hefty bill and a reasonable one, or between a huge hangover and simply feeling good.

In my book (and after all, this *is* my book), the man who really knows the bartending score is Norman Bukofzer, whom everyone simply calls "Norman." You can find him most nights behind the bar at the Ritz-Carlton on New York's Central Park South.

Norman is the most wired bartender I know, and the man I make it a point to see when I am in New York. He is so well connected that he is often invited to celebrity weddings—not to work the bar, but as a guest. That should tell you something about his sphere of power and influence, not to mention his personality. "On a good day, you'll have a drink," Norman laughs. "On a bad day, you'll drink. Either way, the hotel bar is a huge moneymaker."

No one knows more than Norman about what to order and what to avoid, as well as the markup at hotel bars. So what does he recommend that you order at that hotel bar?

- Order a martini or tequila. These are the best bargains in the house because they are almost all alcohol and you're getting the full value of the drink. In fact, one martini at a hotel bar is equivalent to two-and-a-half mixed drinks.

- The alcohol content of gin and tonics and screwdrivers is lower; thus the markup for the hotel is greater.

- The least value in any alcoholic bar drink is a mixed cocktail. But if you must order one, ask for a mojito instead of a cosmopolitan.

- The absolute worst value in any bar drink is a soft drink from a bar that uses a dispensing gun. The hotel bar might charge $2.75 for a Coke, but it costs the hotel only about 3¢ to make.

- Beer is another big-markup item.

Be careful about ordering champagne, wine, and silly drinks from a hotel bar. For example, a bottle of Cristal champagne will run you $125 retail, but a hotel will charge $375—a markup of 200 percent.

Resorts love to advertise frozen tropical drinks. But they are the worst value. They have hardly any alcohol in them, and they may cost $8 to $10. Unless you get a floater top for an extra dollar or two, you are getting very little alcohol in your fancy drink. However, these frozen drinks are the biggest moneymakers for the bar. They cost less than $2 to make. They are also very high in sugar and calories. Most bars use bottled or frozen mixes.

Some hotel bars will even try to market the virgin (nonalcholic) drinks as smoothies but they are made from concentrate and use hardly any fresh fruit at all.

The markup on wine by the bottle is generally three times the hotel's cost. You can pay as much for wine by the glass as you would for a whole bottle of wine. A $6.50 glass of wine might come from a $7 bottle. Want to save money next time you're at a hotel restaurant? Bring your own wine. This is not considered rude. Just call the hotel restaurant and ask whether they have a corkage fee, which usually runs about $10 to $15. At least this way you will be drinking wine you already know you like and you will also be saving money at the same time.

If you choose to drink the hotel restaurant's wine, never order it by the glass. Order the bottle and pay the stiff tariff—if you're dining with friends, this simply makes more sense. There are about four glasses of wine per bottle, so you generally come out ahead that way. And besides, you never know how long that bottle of house wine has been sitting there open.

CHAPTER 11

What Hotel Security Won't Tell You

The traditional definition of hotel security incorporated these simple aims:

- Protect guest rooms from burglary.

- Protect against theft from both employees and guests.

- Investigate fire alarms.

- Keep "undesirables" staying with celebrities out of sight.

- Keep "undesirables" who want to stay with noncelebrities out of the hotel.

- In the event of an emergency, do everything possible not to disturb guests, or (even worse) do everything possible to avoid notifying authorities.

These days, about the only thing most hotel security officials can boast about is that the incidence of thefts from rooms has decreased. But other crimes—robberies, push-in assaults, and terrorism threats—are on the rise.

However, most hoteliers do not want to talk about hotel security. So I will. It's important, and it doesn't have to be a negative.

TERRORISM THREATS AT HOTELS

Since September 11, 2001, the focus of security efforts around the world has been on airports and airlines. And to be sure, the security at both has been tightened.

But what about hotels? A recent study on hotel security by Cornell University's School of Hotel Administration found that many hotels didn't alter their security and safety procedures after September 11. The study revealed that almost 30 percent of general managers had done nothing to improve the security procedures at their hotels, 58 percent had not added security employees, and 25 percent had done nothing to tighten security for their guests.

High-ranking law enforcement authorities told me that they had also informed major hotel chains that a credible terrorist threat existed at many American-branded hotels—Hiltons, Sheratons, Marriotts, Holiday Inns, Hyatts—because some terrorists looked upon these brands as symbols and therefore targets. "To these terrorists," one FBI agent told me, "these hotels are tantamount to the World Trade Center where people spend the night." And perhaps they are even more vulnerable.

A hotel is a terrorist's dream—hundreds of uninspected and unattended bags, multiple entrances and exits, and easy vehicle access. When you consider that terrorists pursue the path of least resistance, you can logically conclude that these American-branded hotels become likely targets.

Nevertheless, most of these hotels have done little or nothing to create an effective, proactive security perimeter around their properties. When I spoke with a number of hotel chain CEOs and asked them what they were doing in this area, I got an almost uniform answer. One CEO told me, "We don't want to do anything to inconvenience our guests." (Isn't this the same argument we would have heard from the major airlines on September 10, 2001?) Another executive insisted that "we have adequate security procedures in place that we can implement at a moment's notice." And when would that moment be? *After* the hotel is bombed? The potential number of casualties is staggering. For example, the Marriott Marquis and the Hilton Hotel in Manhattan are two of the largest hotels in the world. Each has a few thousand rooms and huge ballrooms. Cars drive under-neath these hotels to check in. Any repeat of the 1993 World Trade Center bombing or the explosion at the Federal Build-ing in Oklahoma City at either of these two hotels would be devastating—with the potential loss of life easily exceeding the death toll of September 11.

And yet nothing has been done to prevent this from hap-pening. I could still walk into virtually any hotel in New York—or in the rest of the United States for that matter—with two bags filled with Semtex explosive and tip the bellhop $5 or $10 to watch or store them, and then walk out of the building. I can still drive a huge van up to the front door of the hotel without the vehicle being stopped and inspected. No bags are scanned or inspected.

Overseas, terrorist attacks at a Sheraton in Islamabad and a JW Marriott hotel in Jakarta proved how vulnerable American-branded hotels are. And yet another survey, conducted by John Portman and Associates, an Atlanta-based architect group, found that a staggering 88 percent of travelers surveyed said they are willing to pay more per stay for additional safety and se-curity measures.

So why haven't hotels done more? One answer is that their marketing folks are worried that to do so would be to acknowl-edge a problem and, in the process, frighten thousands of po-tential guests.

But security doesn't have to be a negative. For example, there's the Century Plaza Hotel in Los Angeles. Before the hotel was built in 1964, hotel executives consulted with the U.S. Secret Service, asking the federal agency what it wanted in a se-cure hotel, and then designed the hotel to those standards. (Not surprisingly, every U.S. president since LBJ has stayed there.) The hotel uses this fact and its heightened security to attract guests.

The Century Plaza is the exception to the rule, however.

Most hotels have done nothing to substantially upgrade their security. Some hotels now ask for positive photo I.D. when checking in, and that's about it. Even then, would you believe that nearly 62 percent of business travelers in one survey said that even after showing I.D. they were given keys to an occupied room!

Hotels, like airlines, seem to have a corporate bottom-line culture that will react only *after* a disaster rather than anticipating or preempting one.

So far, we've been very lucky in America. It's a sad comment that it may be a matter of when, not if, terrorists will attack a U.S. hotel in America. And it's my strong position that it won't be until that happens that hotels will take the necessary steps they should be taking now to ensure your safety and security.

Only after a terrible incident—one that more than likely could have been prevented—will you see hotels erect security perimeters around their properties, where all vehicles will have to be inspected at least three hundred feet away from hotel entrances. There will be metal detectors in hotel lobbies, which will require you to enter a hotel much like you now pass through security at an airport, and where your bags will have to be scanned and/or physically inspected before they can be brought to your room. If we now endure this at airports, why shouldn't we take the same precautions at hotels?

But unless or until such an incident happens, there are things you can do to take more control of your own security at hotels:

- If you notice unattended bags in the lobby, report them.

- If you see multiple deliveries being made to one individual hotel room, report it.

- Anytime you see a car parked in front of the lobby, ask management why.

- If you see a "do not disturb" sign hanging from a guest room door for more than twenty-four hours, it is clear that whoever is in there wants to deny access to that room. Other than the obvious exception of the overly amorous honeymoon couple, you should report that as well.

However, the terrorism threat is only the tip of the hotel security iceberg. In fact, there remain numerous cases of security and safety problems at hotels.

HOTEL FIRE SAFETY

Unfortunately, many of these events go unreported to law enforcement because there is no national standard or requirement for hotels to report them to the authorities. Many hotels offer private settlements to plaintiffs rather than allow the public to be aware of specific problems.

Since crime and fire statistics aren't chronicled or organized by authorities as hotel crimes, details are difficult to obtain. However, in the process of researching this book, I was able to successfully cross-reference reported statistics to help paint a picture of what is really going on in terms of hotel fire safety and hotel crime. I also talked to the people who work in hotel security and fire departments, as well as police and law enforcement officials, to help you with your own battle plan for staying safely in hotels.

According to the National Fire Prevention Association, there are an average of about 4,600 hotel or motel fires each year. In 1999, the last year that specific statistics were reported, there were 24 civilian deaths, 249 civilian injuries, and $115 million in property damages. That translates into relatively few fires, and fatality and injury levels are still low. But that doesn't necessarily mean it's been a good period for hotel fire safety. In many cases, we've just been lucky.

In 1946, the worst hotel fire in U.S. history happened at the Winecoff Hotel in Atlanta, when 119 people died. In November 1980, a hotel employee discovered a fire in the unoccupied deli area of the MGM Grand Hotel in Las Vegas. The fire department was notified and an announcement was made over the public address system to evacuate the casino area. However, the fire was moving so rapidly that it quickly reached a "flashover" stage in the deli and spread throughout the casino. The heat and smoke extended through elevator shafts and stairways through twenty-one floors of the hotel. The fire resulted in 85 fatalities and injured 778 guests and 7 hotel employees. One month later, 26 people died in a fire at the Stouffer's Inn in New York. And in February 1981, only three months after the MGM fire, the Las Vegas Hilton was the site of another major fire, where 8 people died and more than 600 people were injured. And then there was the New Year's Eve fire of 1986 at the Dupont Plaza Hotel in San Juan, which killed 97 people in the course of just twelve minutes! Indeed, the 1970s and 1980s registered the greatest number of hotel fire fatalities—more than 400 deaths in multistory hotel fires.

It wasn't until 1990 that the Hotel and Motel Fire Safety Act was passed into law by Congress, which then required the installation of hardwired smoke detectors in each guest room and an automatic sprinkler system (with a sprinkler head in each guest room) in any hotel taller than three stories. This was a step in the right direction. Still, a disturbing majority of hotel guests have no idea how to protect themselves in the event of a fire— or even how to safely escape a burning hotel.

Much of the blame can be assessed against outdated city and state fire codes. This fact, combined with a historic unwillingness on the part of many hotels (and chains) to upgrade their fire safety systems, has led to a number of well-documented tragedies.

Not surprisingly, the worst record for fire prevention and fire safety methods is held at resort and convention areas, especially where high-rise buildings are involved. The substandard fire codes in Las Vegas had long been detailed in the wake of the tragic MGM Grand Hotel fire. (And since then, as a direct result of the tragedy, the Nevada fire codes have been strengthened.)

A few thousand miles away, however, in Honolulu, an overwhelming number of hotels were built without sprinkler systems or smoke or heat detectors. And it was a major legislative fight to get these hotels to retrofit, even after the Las Vegas disaster.

Strange as this may seem, some hotels are more concerned about inconveniencing their guests than they are about promptly responding to alarms. They don't call the fire department until a fire is actually confirmed. This policy can cause precious minutes to be lost. (An important tip: if you hear a hotel fire alarm sound in your room or in the hallway, that doesn't mean the hotel has notified authorities. You should pick up the phone, call 911, and report it directly yourself.)

When the MGM Grand was rebuilt in Las Vegas, its new computer-controlled fire safety system focused on the detection and removal of smoke. (Investigations following the 1980 fire showed that more than sixty of the eighty-five victims died of carbon monoxide poisoning from smoke that swept quickly through the building.)

Many hotels have recently installed one of the more advanced fire safety systems, complete with automatic sprinklers in all public, private, and service areas; smoke detectors and speakers in each guest room for direct communication to all guests by the fire department; headsets for two-way communication with the fire department at each "pull" (alarm) station; and automatic and manual smoke exhaust systems.

Ultimately, a strict building code is only part of the solution. Furniture, drapes, carpets, and other materials are often constructed of materials that greatly add to the toxicity of the smoke. In addition, there is an ongoing argument about the cost savings of polyvinyl chloride (PVC) versus the danger of its burning or smoking. PVC is widely used in new hotel construction for electrical wiring and plumbing.

Short of demanding a room on a lower floor, which may or may not protect you, there is certain must-know information you should consider a prerequisite to a night's lodging.

First, take two minutes to check out the floor plan of your room, as well as the hall on the floor where you're staying. Locate the position of the stairs, *not* the location of the elevators. You can't, and shouldn't, count on an elevator in a fire emergency. Is there a fire alarm in the hall? If so, does it sound only at the front desk or in the whole building, and does it automatically call the fire department?

Once a fire is discovered, many firefighters suggest that you do everything you possibly can to get out of your room. First, drop to the floor. Stay on your knees below what you assess to be the smoke line. Most people who die in fires are first knocked out by—then killed by—the smoke. If you simply jump out of bed and stand up at the sound of a fire alarm or if you smell smoke, it could be a deadly move. Don't open the hotel door. Instead, check the door by feeling it with your hands. If it feels very hot, don't open it at all. Stay in your room. Shut off the air conditioner (in a fire, the air conditioner could suck smoke from a lower floor into the room), stuff a wet towel under the door, and remove all the drapes from the window. Next, head for the bathroom. Fill the tub with water . . . and wait.

If, however, the room door doesn't feel hot, then, staying on your knees *before* opening it, crawl out the door and head for the nearest stairway. While moving to the exit, keep close to the walls. Chances are, it will be dark and/or smoky.

Should the stairwell start filling with thick smoke, head back to your room, or, if that's not possible, head for the roof.

Here are some other tips to protect yourself:

- Do not stay in a hotel that is not equipped with automatic fire sprinklers and guest room smoke detectors throughout the building.

Many buildings are still not in compliance with modern codes because of "grandfathering," a policy whereby codes are not required to be retroactively applied. Even when good codes are on the books, enforcement may be hurt by a scarcity of resources in building and fire departments or by the existence of huge loopholes. Some countries, for example, require sprinkler systems and smoke detectors for any hotels of more than sixty units. And yet a number of three-hundred-room hotels don't have them because the owners of these hotels cleverly sell off portions of the hotel to other owners in lots of fifty-nine units. A hotel either has the sprinklers and detectors or it doesn't. "We're in compliance with all building codes" is not a satisfactory answer.

- Make it a habit to pack and then place a small flashlight on your nightstand in case of a power outage due to fire or other emergencies.

HOTEL CRIME

Because the police departments in major cities do not keep specific data on hotel crime and hotels keep the incidents quiet, crimes in hotels are a closely held secret. Still, about ten thousand security-related lawsuits are filed against hotels each year. Here are some New York City examples:

- A man with a rap sheet for push-in robberies was caught hiding in a maid's closet at Manhattan's Sheraton Hotel, hoping to pounce on unsuspecting guests.

- Con men robbed an $80,000 gem from a diamond dealer staying in the Waldorf-Astoria.

- A Canadian businesswoman suffered a broken jaw during a push-in robbery at the Paramount Hotel on West 46th Street. She was followed to her room by convicted felons, who grabbed her from behind. Records showed there had been at least twenty-three people arrested at the Paramount between 1986 and 1998 for assault, weapons possession, attempted robbery, larceny, drugs, and burglary.

- A woman was raped at knifepoint at the Hotel Pennsylvania in a mezzanine-level bathroom in 1995. This hotel had logged seventeen petty larcenies, twenty-one grand larcenies, twelve burglaries, and one attempted robbery in 1994 alone. Although the hotel—under new ownership—says security has been increased, access to the hotel floors was easily accomplished by this writer.

- A UCLA history professor lost a lawsuit against the Waldorf-Astoria over a sexual assault that allegedly took place when a stranger broke into her room during the night. In the previous ten years there had been at least sixty arrests for robbery, larceny, burglary, sexual assault, and homicide. At the time, reporters were able to easily access guest room floors despite the hotel's claim of a high level of security.

- A Florida businesswoman who had just checked into the Roosevelt Hotel was pushed into her room from behind and beaten. The assailant attempted rape until she screamed that she had AIDS. Before fleeing, he ransacked the room for valuables.

Here are some additional case studies:

On March 10, 2000, a businesswoman staying in a Marriott hotel, was pushed into her room as she exited to meet colleagues for breakfast. She screamed loudly, and the commotion caused a guest from another room to call security. Security guards arrived at the door to the room to hear the woman say, "Please don't kill me!" and a man's voice responding, "Shut up, bitch, or I'm going to kill you." Struggle continued, and he began to sodomize her. Security officers decided not to intervene, but instead went to a security phone on that floor. They discovered, however, that the phone was inoperable because it did not have a phone cord!

After a delay of several minutes, one officer radioed the Marriott operator to call for police assistance. He did not communicate the gravity of the situation because he was afraid other guests would be alarmed. The operator misidentified the information to the police by saying that there was a domestic dispute going on in the room. While waiting for the police, the security officers saw the assailant exit the room, step on the elevator, and casually walk out of the hotel, holding a washcloth to his bleeding face. They still did not intervene.

Marriott officials testified that their security cameras did not capture a picture of the assailant. Fifty-four days later he was apprehended, and it was discovered that the assailant was HIV positive and had infected the woman. A jury awarded the plaintiff $8.7 million.

In August 1993 a young woman was murdered by strangulation in her hotel room at a Holiday Inn in Des Moines, Iowa. Investigators found no forced entry into the room and surmised that since she had been a guest there for ten days due to a job relocation, she must have known her killer and voluntarily let the person into the room. Therefore, the initial investigation focused on those people she had contact with prior to her death.

It was not until 1999 that sophisticated DNA analysis linked the chief engineer of the hotel to the murder. The chief engineer had continual access to the "E" key (which can override a dead bolt) and the master keys. He had been hired by the property without receiving a background check and was retained on staff despite his previous history of sexually harassing and physically abusing female employees. Even though he had resigned right before the young woman was murdered, he still frequented the hotel and lingered in the employees' lounge.

In 2000 he was charged and linked with DNA evidence to the murder. However, police had notified the plaintiff in June of 1999 that this man was a suspect, and it was not publicized until January 2000 that the murderer was a former employee of the hotel. The statute of limitations had by then run out and, therefore, the survivors' case was denied.

On November 14, 2002, a young woman was murdered in her Hampton Inn room by the maintenance manager who had access to master keys for the hotel. He entered her room through the adjoining room and bludgeoned her to death. He had a previous criminal history, and the crime would have been prevented if the hotel had performed a prehire background check.

These are just a few hotel crime stories—and every one of these terrible incidents could have been prevented. In many cases, these hotels (like thousands of others) were equipped with multiple closed-circuit television (CCTV) cameras. But having the cameras doesn't mean that they are working or that someone is constantly monitoring them.

I asked officials of SafePlace, a Wilmington, Delaware, corporation (www.safeplace.com) that evaluates hotels against specific security, fire protection, and health and safety requirements, to compile a list of essential ways for hotel guests to protect themselves:

- Never open the door if you are not expecting anyone, and make sure that there is no one lurking around your room before you open the door.

THE INFAMOUS PEEPHOLE CASE:
The peephole on your guest room door may not be the only peephole in your room. Consider the case of two Holiday Inn hotels—one in Walterborough, South Carolina, and another in Cleveland, Tennessee. The South Carolina Holiday Inn franchise faced five lawsuits from guests claiming that they were watched by hotel employees through peepholes in bedrooms and bathrooms. A similar charge was filed against the Tennessee Holiday Inn. The South Carolina cases were ultimately settled for $500,000 (even though a jury returned a verdict of $10 million).

Holiday Inn franchisees were then required to sign an affidavit certifying that their properties were peephole-free.

But how do you know whether there are any additional peepholes in your guest room? You don't. However, here are a few things to take notice of. Beware of connecting doors between rooms. If your connecting door has a peephole, make sure it looks out, not in. If you discover a desilvered mirror in your room, ask to move to another room.

- Always use your view port when opening the door. Open your door only to persons known to you. An unexpected visit from hotel staff should be verified with the front desk before opening the door.

- Do not place the in-room breakfast menu on your door at night. This sends a clear message that there is a single person in the room.

- Never prop your hotel room door open. When closing the door, always use the dead bolt, as well as a chain lock if one is available. (To its credit, in 1995, AAA made the installation of dead-bolt locks in every room a requirement for a hotel to be inspected and rated. The specific requirement: each room must have a primary lock that permits the guest to lock the door when leaving the room. Then it must have a dead-bolt lock that cannot be opened from the outside with a guest room or master key when locked by the guest from the inside.)

• If there is an adjoining room, ensure that the door locks via a dead bolt accessible only from inside your room. If there is no dead bolt, by all means, ask for another room. If this is the only room available and the door opens into your room, you may also want to place something heavy in front of the door so that no one can enter the room by force.

Some of the best ways for travelers to assure themselves that they are staying in a secure hotel and that there are proper procedures and safety features in place are to simply not be afraid to ask questions, do a little inspection on their own, and stay alert while away from home.

Before booking your hotel, you should ask these questions:

• Has your hotel been reviewed by an independent third-party company for security and safety features?

• Does the hotel employ twenty-four-hour security personnel? (In many cases, a hotel will say they do have twenty-four-hour security, when, in fact, the security staff might consist of only the hotel engineer or maintenance person. Also, is the security officer an employee of the hotel or someone working for a subcontractor?

• Does the hotel require proof of identification of all guests?

- Is access to guest room floors restricted to resident guests with valid electronic key cards only?

- Do all of the hotel rooms and common areas have working fire sprinklers and smoke detectors?

- How many incidents of burglary and other crimes are there each year at the hotel?

- Are there in-room safes or another hotel safe in which to store valuables?

- Does the hotel perform prehire criminal background checks on employees?

It is important to remember that price, reputation for impeccable hospitality services, and brand name do not necessarily indicate a safe hotel. If you are uncomfortable with any of the answers to the preceding questions, do not hesitate to probe further and ask them what they are doing to improve their attention to these important details. It is your money and, more important, your safety. You have the right not to stay there and to choose to stay in a safer hotel.

In examining a hotel's security and safety, it is important to remember that all guests have the responsibility for their own safety as well. There are certain things that travelers can do to protect themselves before they embark on a trip, as well as during their stay. Many of these are based on common sense, although others are not—but they are all important and may someday save you, even if you are unaware of it.

Before you leave on a trip:

- Always leave a travel itinerary with someone at home, at work, or with a relative or trusted friend. This allows others to contact you in case of an emergency at home, and ensures that someone knows where you are in case there is an incident at the location where you are staying.

After hotel check-in:

- Once you arrive at your destination, call home or work to let them know you have arrived safely and notify them whether there are any changes in your itinerary.

- When entering your room for the first time, ask the bellhop to remain while you perform your room security check. Close the door directly behind you when he leaves.

- When you leave your hotel room for the day or evening, leave the television on. From outside the room it sounds like the room is occupied.

- You should also place the "do not disturb" sign on your door. The sign gives the impression that you are in the room when you are not.

- Call housekeeping for maid service and instruct them to leave the sign on the door. Never use the "clean the room" sign, which signals that you are out of the room.

Some hotels are taking proactive stances and flagging the rooms of guests who do not allow the housekeepers to access their rooms for several days. This is in direct response to certain instances of covert and illegal activities and should not be taken personally. For this reason, it is imperative that you *do* contact housekeeping to clean your room.

ADULTPROOFING YOUR ROOM

No one knows how a twenty-one-year-old college student fell from the balcony of an eighth-floor hotel room in Cancún in 2000, but investigators have a pretty good idea of what contributed to the fatal plunge. Mexican law allows hotel balcony railings to be substantially lower than the legal minimum in the United States—and tourists in Mexican resort cities die in falls from hotel balconies with surprising frequency.

Since 1978, at least forty-nine foreigners have been killed in falls from those balconies. In the United States, hotel balconies must be at least forty-two inches high. In Mexico, some are as low as two feet—clearly unacceptable. But people check into these rooms every day.

My advice: when checking into your room, take a good look around, then a good walk around—not just inside the room, but also out on the balcony. And this does not just apply in Mexico. If you're uncomfortable with the height of the balcony railing, move some furniture against it.

Because of these problems, the U.S. Department of State has recently begun making this information part of its Consular Information Sheets, which are available to all travelers. Also, in the case of Mexico, the United States now warns citizens about balcony deaths (visit http://travel.state.gov/mexico.html).

Another potential hazard is electrical outlets. Newer hotels try to keep most of them away from sinks, showers, and bathtubs in bathrooms. Still, it's your responsibility to choose common sense over convenience.

CHILDPROOFING YOUR ROOM

An overwhelming number of security and safety issues at hotels involve families traveling with children. Swimming pools, balconies, and many other potential hazards await at every hotel.

The U.S. Consumer Products and Safety Commission (CPSC) reports that about 2.5 million children are injured or killed by hazards in the home each year—and some of these accidents also happen in hotel rooms. The good news is that many of these incidents can be prevented by using simple child safety devices that are on the market today.

If you're traveling with young children, there are some hotels that do an excellent job of childproofing your room (if you inform them ahead of time). An example is the Four Seasons hotel in Maui. On the day of arrival, the housekeeping department childproofs the room according to the children's ages. For each room with toddlers, this includes soft bumpers around all tables in the room, mesh screens on the lanai railings so little arms and heads can't fit through the spaces, covers over the light sockets on all electrical outlets, soft covers over the tub faucets, and small toddler beds built low to the floor with side rails.

In Boston, the Ritz-Carlton has childproofed its Junior Presidential Suite. The windows will not open higher than two inches, all electrical outlets are covered, shelf corners are protected, a safety partition is built into the corner bed, the water is temperature controlled to prevent scalding, materials are flame retardant, and toys were chosen according to government safety regulations.

But these two hotels are clearly the exception. The responsibility rests with you. When you check into a hotel room, and before your child is even allowed into the room, get on your knees and scout the room at child level. Look for all electrical outlets, sharp edges, and doorways. Move toiletries and drinking glasses. Also tie up window blind cords to keep them out of your kids' reach.

If you're traveling with very young children, there's an additional problem: the cribs that many hotels provide. Each year, about forty babies suffocate or strangle in their cribs when they become trapped between broken crib parts or in cribs with older, unsafe designs. Soft bedding such as quilts, comforters, and pillows can suffocate a baby. As many as three thousand infants die each year from sudden infant death syndrome (SIDS) and up to one-third of these cases may have been the result of suffocation by the soft bedding.

Estimates show that children under age two spend more than seven million nights per year in hotels, motels, and resorts. Many traveling families use cribs and play yards provided by motels and hotels. Recent spot checks, however, found unsafe cribs and play yards in 80 percent of the hotels and motels visited.

The inspection included ninety hotels and motels in twenty-seven states and the District of Columbia. Of the regular cribs inspected, 82 percent had at least one safety hazard, including loose hardware or unsecured mattress supports, which could entrap a baby; soft bedding, including quilts, comforters, or pillows that could cause suffocation; and adult-sized sheets that pose a strangulation and suffocation hazard. Of the play yards and mesh cribs inspected, 52 percent had at least one safety hazard, including tears or holes in the mesh, which pose an entrapment risk to babies, and soft bedding.

The CPSC recommends that a baby under twelve months old be put to sleep in a crib on his or her back with no soft bedding. Adult sheets should never be used in a crib because they pose a strangulation and suffocation risk to babies. Hotels and motels should provide fitted crib sheets in good condition that fit the mattress securely.

If you want complete information, as well as the recall list, call the CPSC hotline at (800) 638-2772. You can also get the information on the Web (or report crib problems at particular hotels) at www.cpsc.gov.

If you're at a resort that has duplexes, or you're in a ground-floor room with easy access to a pool, ask the hotel to provide a safety gate to help prevent falls down stairs and to keep children away from dangerous areas.

Bring your own doorknob covers and door locks to help prevent children from entering rooms and other areas with possible dangers, such as swimming pools. Be sure the doorknob cover is sturdy enough not to break but allows a door to be opened quickly by an adult in case of emergency. By restricting access to potentially hazardous rooms in the home, doorknob covers could help prevent many kinds of injuries. To prevent access to swimming pools, door locks should be placed high, out of reach of young children. Locks should be used in addition to fences and door alarms. Sliding glass doors in a first-floor hotel room, with locks that must be resecured after each use, may not be an effective barrier to a pool.

If you're staying in a room that's higher than the first floor and it has a balcony, ask the hotel to provide sturdy safety netting to help prevent falls from windows, balconies, decks, and landings. There should be no more than four inches between the bars of a window or balcony guard.

Ask the hotel to provide corner and edge bumpers to help prevent injuries from falls against sharp edges of furniture and fireplaces. These bumpers do a great job of softening falls against those sharp or rough edges. Or better yet, bring your own.

Even more important, bring along outlet covers and outlet plates. You can never have enough (and most hotels don't have these on hand) to help prevent shock and possible electrocution.

HOTEL THEFT

The maid at the Kahala Hilton in Honolulu (now the Kahala Mandarin) thought it was a little strange when she went to clean one of the rooms at the posh resort.

The room was virtually empty, except for an odd combination of objects on the dresser—a few wallets, some watches, a large set of keys. That wasn't particularly strange, except that the bed was made. No one had slept in the room the night before. The bathroom was also unused. But the toilet had been flushed, and something was floating in the water. Curious, she looked in the basin and saw some torn identification cards and a driver's license: Mr. Gary Ross.

She immediately called the front desk. She told the clerk the number of the room she was in and reported that a "Mr. Ross" had apparently discarded his license by mistake. She then resumed her cleaning chores.

Less than a minute later, the phone rang in the room. "What did you say the guest's name was?" asked the man at the front desk. "Ross," she replied.

There was no Ross registered at the hotel. And whoever *was* registered in that room had not yet checked out. Security was notified and came quickly to the room.

Within minutes, the hotel's security officer was on the phone to other hotel security chiefs, trying to cross-reference the Ross name. Soon, the Hawaiian Regent Hotel called him back. The day before, a man named Gary Ross had reported to police the theft of several of his belongings—including his wallet—from his room at the Regent.

The police were summoned. In the meantime, the man who was staying in that room made the mistake of returning. The detectives asked him if he knew a Gary Ross. He replied that he didn't. In fact, at first the police thought this man had also been victimized because of the general condition of the room.

Then, one of the detectives noticed something peculiar on the dresser. One of the objects clearly matched what had been reported stolen earlier that day from the Hawaiian Regent.

The "guest," a man later identified as Richard Carl Rex, age thirty-six, was then arrested by Honolulu police and charged with passkey theft. What made the arrest interesting is that the police were convinced that Rex was part of "the Miami Group," an internationally known gang of master hotel thieves. (Although the link was never substantiated, evidence found in Rex's hotel room included eight master keys to another major Waikiki hotel.)

YOUR HOTEL KEY CARD: Never underestimate the Internet's ability to frighten the hell out of travelers. An e-mail making the rounds claims that California law enforcement agencies are probing what hotels encode on the programmable card keys that operate guest room locks. The claim is that hotels are placing guests' credit card numbers and other sensitive information on the magnetic stripes of card keys and that unscrupulous hotel employees are using card readers to steal the identities of travelers.

Southern California law enforcement professionals assigned to detect new threats to personal security issues, recently discovered what type of information is embedded in the credit card type hotel room keys used throughout the industry.

Although room keys differ from hotel to hotel, a key obtained from one well-known hotel chain that was being used for a regional Identity Theft Presentation was found to contain the following information:
a. Customer's (your) name
b. Customer's partial home address
c. Hotel room number
d. Check-in date and checkout date
e. Customer's (your) credit card number and expiration date!

When you turn them in to the front desk your personal information is there for any employee to access by simply scanning the card in the hotel scanner. An employee can take a handful of cards home and, using a scanning device, access the information onto a laptop computer and go shopping at your expense.

Simply put, hotels do not erase these cards until an employee issues the card to the next hotel guest. It is usually kept in a drawer at the front desk with YOUR INFORMATION ON IT!!!!

The bottom line is, keep the cards or destroy them! NEVER leave them behind and NEVER turn them in to the front desk when you check out of a room. They should not charge you for the card.

Well, there is a kernel of truth in this e-mail somewhere. Hotels do have the capacity to encode virtually anything on a card key. But almost none of them put anything more than check-in and checkout times on the cards. If you're concerned, take the easy way out: don't return the card key to the front desk when you check out. Hotels couldn't care less whether you return them.

Rex was extradited to California on another charge. And the real Gary Ross was reunited with what was left of his wallet.

There isn't one city in the United States that doesn't have a sizable hotel burglary problem—and a large part of that problem is the guests themselves. After all, you would never leave the door unlocked at home or leave the keys to your house or car lying around. Somehow, when people check into a hotel, they forget the rules. They almost invite a rip-off.

Some incidents involve crimes of distraction, with groups of criminals working in pairs. For the most part, a new hotel guest is in trouble from the moment he arrives. Just as you're checking in, one of the gang members may squirt a hidden bottle of catsup or mustard on your suit. While one is 'helping' you wipe it off, the other is also stealing your wallet.

If you're checking into a hotel that caters to conventions and large groups, you need to pay particular attention to your luggage, unless all the luggage is chained together. Lately, room burglars have gotten smart: they won't take all your credit cards; they'll take just one on the hunch that you won't miss it for a few days. And in a very short period of time, they'll bang it up to your maximum credit line.

Protecting room number distribution also didn't stop one crafty thief, who came attired in a chauffeur's uniform. He entered the hotel lobby, walked to the gift shop, and bought a cheap greeting card. On the envelope he wrote the name of the guest he wanted to rip off. Then, he simply walked up to the front desk and politely asked the room clerk whether he could deliver the gift himself. He got the room number he wanted.

To be sure, none of the hotels I spoke with would confirm any room burglary figures. And, as with hotel fire safety and terrorism, you once again need to take more control of your own security.

Women hotel guests can be particularly vulnerable. A criminal waiting in the lobby can get on the elevator with a woman, wait for her to push a button for her floor first, then push the button for the floor directly above her, and double back to the woman's floor.

Many guests don't use their dead bolts or security latches. Dead bolts and chains are also effective in keeping guests *in*— sleepwalkers tend to walk out of doors (thinking they are going to the bathroom) if they aren't bolted. There's not a hotel general manager who didn't report to me cases of embarrassed and naked male and female guests in hotel hallways at three in the morning, who had locked themselves out of their rooms. Each had been trying to get to the bathroom, but because they hadn't used the dead bolt, they didn't notice, in their sleepy stupor, that they were using the wrong door.

In all seriousness, part of your security plan must include direct communication with the hotel. San Francisco attorney Alexander Anolik recently suggested an up-front yet subtle approach to protecting your room and your belongings.

One of the signature behaviors of hotel room thieves is to go for the path of least resistance. Many of them figure that if you act like you own the room, no one will challenge you, especially the maids. Here's a typical scenario. A hotel burglar walks the halls of a large city hotel, looking for the maid cart outside suites. He (although some burglars are female) finds a suite where the maid is clearly inside by noticing one of two things: either a card hanging on the outside doorknob announcing "maid service" (the maid is in the room) or, even better, the door is ajar. He then simply walks into the room and announces his presence to the maid, taking off an outer jacket and heading to the bedroom. "Don't worry about me," the thief says, nonchalantly, and throws the jacket onto the bed or armchair. He then starts to act busy—picking up the phone, perhaps even making some calls.

The maid assumes that this is indeed the person who belongs in that room and continues her duties. While she cleans the bathroom, the thief loots the bedroom, then he looks for jewelry on bathroom counters while the maid is in the bedroom.

Anolik advises that whenever you are staying at a hotel for more than one night, you should do the following before leaving your room in the morning. Call housekeeping and ask for the person in charge. Get the name and title of the person to whom you speak, and give that person your name and room number. Then explain that you want to inform the maid assigned to cleaning your room that no one is to be allowed inside the room while she is there.

This sends two important messages to the maid without being heavy-handed or accusatory. The first is that no one—no matter who they say they are—can come into your room while she is cleaning it. The second is a subliminal message that the room will probably be thoroughly checked after the maid has left it.

Of course, no one can discount the amount of stuff stolen from guest rooms—by the guests themselves!

WHAT PEOPLE STEAL

What's your best memory of a favorite hotel? Great service? A room with a terrific view? A romantic meal? Or is it that ashtray you pocketed, the extra bath towel or bathrobe you took with you, the extra bar of soap or that pair of slippers that somehow found their way into your suitcase?

Be honest, and admit it. Chances are reasonably good that if you've ever stayed in a hotel, you've taken something more than just your bill with you when you left. Most of us, at least one time in our lives, have been part of the charge of the light-fingered brigade.

There's a very good reason why most hotel room television sets are bolted to the wall; there's an equally good reason why hotel room bed boards, paintings, lamps, and even soap dishes are fastened tight. "People will steal just about anything not secured," says one hotel manager. "And I mean anything."

The fact that many guests steal articles from the hotels where they are staying is not exactly a news bulletin. But what they are taking these days may surprise you. Would you believe hotel telephones, entire room carpets, bathroom fixtures, and marble fireplaces? These are just some of the items that have been lifted by guests.

Most hotel managers will tell you that losing things like ashtrays comes with the territory. Some European hotels—where smoking is still permitted—replace about eight thousand ashtrays a year.

When the InterContinental London opened in June 1975, management fully expected certain items to vanish. Indeed, dozens of ashtrays, towels, and bathrobes checked out of the hotel. But hotel officials were clearly surprised when a guest not only checked out with his luggage but had also taken his bathroom door.

Then there was the case of the missing Egyptian bidet faucets. At the Ramses Hilton in Cairo, when the general manager investigated the mysterious disappearance, he discovered the culprit—a Japanese bathroom accessory manufacturer.

The headboards in most of the rooms at the Hilton in Malta once contained eight-pointed Maltese crosses. Then the guests filed off the crosses and took them from the rooms.

In Dubai, one hotel guest who had been staying there until he could move into a more permanent residence invited the manager to dinner in his new apartment. "The minute I walked in I saw it," says the manager. "The hotel had furnished his entire apartment—china, glasses, silverware, paintings, and even seat cushions. I was too dumbstruck to say anything at dinner."

Sometimes, when hotel management adds a new item to a guest room, they fully expect it to disappear. A few years ago in New York, when a large hotel added giant bath sheets to guest bathrooms, the hotel prepared for a mass exodus of the huge towels. It never happened. The towels were so large people just couldn't get them in their suitcases. However, they did lose an awful lot of expensive washcloths.

In fact, washcloths and small hand towels are the number one item stolen from guest rooms today. People use them to wrap, insulate, and protect items in their bags.

Here's a wild statistic. It's estimated that seven out of ten American adults have stayed at least once in a Holiday Inn. And nine out of ten of those people admit to taking one of those trademark green-and-white Holiday Inn towels with them. Are you surprised?

In current terms, this means the Holiday Inn folks lose about 590,000 towels *a year!* Recently, the hotel staged a special "towel amnesty" day, asking people to either return one of the "borrowed" towels or at the very least share with the hotel the different ways they used their Holiday Inn towel. In return, they would receive a brand-new green-and-white towel.

It's unknown how many people responded to this public relations tactic. But what was fascinating was the admission from Holiday Inns of the number of towels the chain loses each year.

Few hotels lose that many bathrobes these days, however. One reason for this is that the quality of many hotel bathrobes is not what it used to be. And besides, who was the idiot who sold hotels on the idea that when it comes to bathrobes one size fits all? It doesn't!

Nevertheless, some guests will take just about anything. Some take because they actually think they need the item. Others are more, uh, "serious collectors," such as Jean Francois Vernetti, the collector of "do not disturb" signs (see Chapter 7).

Most hotels don't get upset when the "do not disturb" signs end up in your luggage. In many cases, the hotel name and logo are displayed prominently on the sign, and hotels presume that you will, in essence, be advertising their hotel if you display the sign. It's when the items taken are somewhat larger that the hotels get hit hard.

At the Beverly Wilshire Hotel, one guest stopped just short of taking the bathroom sink. In past years, the hotel had expensive paintings stolen from guest rooms. Many of the Oriental scatter rugs placed on guest room floors disappeared as well. The hotel replaced them and had them sewn to the floor. They disappeared again.

Sometimes a hotel unwittingly helps in a theft. When a Beverly Wilshire bellhop arrived at a suite to help a guest check out, the man was waiting with his suitcases—and the room's marble fireplace that he had just cut and chiseled out of the wall. "Just taking it to get repaired," said the guest nonchalantly. The bellhop helped him take the fireplace out of the hotel. The guest and the fireplace were never seen again.

Sometimes a hotel gets lucky. A guest staying at the Cavalieri Hilton in Rome ordered all his meals through room service, and he ordered the food according to the cutlery he needed. When he had put together a complete service for eight, he checked out. But the hotel had been keeping track of the missing silverware, and all of it was discreetly removed from his luggage before he left.

When the staff at the Beverly Wilshire noticed a sterling silver coffee pot missing from the room of a guest who had just left to check out, they notified the manager, who raced downstairs to intercept him. "We're so pleased you liked the pot," he told the startled guest. "And because you're a regular with us, instead of charging you our cost of $150 for it, we'll only charge you $75." The man reached deep into his luggage, retrieved the pot, and slammed it down on the checkout counter. "Not worth it," he said.

Every once in a while, stolen hotel goodies return after the fact. There's the legendary story of the Hilton Hotel in Abidjan, on the Ivory Coast. One day the manager of the hotel received a large, unexpected cardboard package from the United States. When worried security officers opened the box, they found a tremendous amount of the hotel's silverware. An accompanying letter explained that the guest had accumulated the utensils during many stays, had felt guilty, and thus was forking over the large quantity of spoons, knives, and, yes, forks. He begged the Ivory Coast Hilton to "grant its forgiveness and thus cleanse my soul."

It is not surprising that a growing number of hotels are removing their names and logos from just about everything. Whatever remains with a logo is a target for theft. At one hotel, executives were convinced they had stopped the theft problem when they took the logos off towels, robes, ashtrays, and coat hangers. And then their ice buckets started walking out with guests. You guessed it—they had forgotten to remove the logos.

During the renovation of one hotel, construction workers hung twelve Victorian painted wooden characters holding signs reading "Please excuse our dust." All twelve were stolen. Even the hotel's wooden room numbers, directional signs, and the shell in each bathroom that held amenities disappeared.

One hotel in Miami has come to expect that hundreds of washcloths will vanish in any given month. The reason: "We get a lot of South American guests who purchase electronic goodies while they are here in the States," says the general manager. "And one of the common things we find is that they like to use our washcloths as shock absorbers to protect the electronics from the flight back home. We go through at least ten thousand washcloths a year."

But the fun is just beginning. Apparently so many guests steal so many items that it is no longer unusual for guests to leave behind a few items they've stolen at one hotel when they check out at a different hotel! One item that is frequently taken is hair dryers.

WHAT PEOPLE LEAVE IN HOTEL ROOMS

OK, so what items do people leave in hotel rooms? Everything from an entire collection of ripped La Perla lingerie to false teeth, from inflatable sex toys to an occasional live barnyard animal.

Hoteliers have learned the hard way how to handle lost items they've found. Rule number one: they will *never* mail them back without first asking you, for a number of obvious reasons. More often they will contact you to let you know that you may have left something of value in your hotel room, and then they will wait for you to suggest what that item might be.

As I already mentioned, the number one item left in hotel rooms is cell phone chargers. Other items that are frequently left behind include women's wristwatches (apparently women hotel guests frequently travel with more than one watch), sunglasses, and sexual devices and lingerie.

CHAPTER 12

Rooms with a Past

Room 902 at the Amsterdam Hilton. Room 311 at the Givenchy Resort in Palm Springs. Room 100 at the Chelsea Hotel in New York. Room 511 at the Vista Hotel in Washington, D.C. What do these and countless other rooms have in common? Good, bad, and sometimes even ugly, these are hotel rooms with a past. Each room is loaded with colorful history, scandal, shame, or pure idiosyncracy. And, without exception, each is available for anyone to spend the night.

FAMOUS (OR INFAMOUS) HOTEL ROOM HISTORIES

Amsterdam Hilton, Room 902, The Netherlands

Every generation produces romantic couples who mesmerize the public. In the late 1960s, none felt the worldwide glare of the press more than Beatle John Lennon and Yoko Ono, who was at that time his girlfriend. The two had met in London in November 1966 at an exhibition of Ono's performance art. Many subsequently blamed Ono for the breakup of the Beatles, which became official with the group's last public appearance in January 1969.

On March 20, 1969, the couple wed in Gibraltar. The following week, the two master media manipulators used their celebrity for good, hosting a honeymoon "bed-in" for peace in room 902, the presidential suite of the Amsterdam Hilton. The press avidly pursued them, assuming that the famous exhibitionists would make love for their cameras. Instead, the pajama-clad newlyweds spoke out about world peace. It was the honeymoon as performance art, interlaced with protest against the Vietnam War. And they painted the entire hotel room *white*.

Lennon's "The Ballad of John and Yoko" chronicles the week

in song. During that time, John and Yoko gave interviews, ignoring the mockery and hostility, to spread their words of peace to a global audience.

In mid-May, the couple planned to mount a second bed-in, this time in New York. Authorities at the U.S. embassy in London refused to issue Lennon a visa because of an earlier marijuana arrest. So on May 24, 1969, John and Yoko flew to the Bahamas. John found the island too hot and humid to stay in bed there for a week, and they abruptly left.

The newlyweds headed north, taking corner-suite rooms 1738-40-42 at the stately Queen Elizabeth Hotel in Montreal on May 26, 1969, to stage their second weeklong bed-in for peace.

On June 1, 1969, the call went out for recording equipment. John and Yoko, along with a roomful of people who included sixties guru Dr. Timothy Leary, Montreal rabbi Abraham Feinberg, Beatles press agent Derek Taylor, singer Petula Clark, and members of the Canadian Radha Krishna Temple as the chorus, recorded "Give Peace a Chance." The single is credited to "The Plastic Ono Band." Five weeks later, on July 7, the 45 record was released in the United States. "Give Peace a Chance" reached number fourteen on Billboard's pop music chart—and inspired an entire generation to chant a song of peace along with John and Yoko.

Greyfield Inn, Cumberland Island, Georgia

John Kennedy Jr., who won the hearts of America as a toddler in the White House and who grew up to be labeled the nation's most gorgeous bachelor, met Carolyn Bessette when she was a public relations executive with Calvin Klein in New York. They began dating in 1994 and moved in together in 1995.

On September 21, 1996, they married at the tiny African Baptist Church chapel on Cumberland Island off the Georgia coast. The reception was held at the Greyfield Inn, a secluded bed-and-breakfast establishment on the island, which is accessible only by boat. A lot of people went to great lengths to keep the event secret, and the ploy worked, as the media were widely caught off guard. Kennedy and his new wife stayed at the inn for a portion of their honeymoon.

San Ysidro Ranch, California

First introduced at a May 1951 Georgetown dinner party, John F. Kennedy and Jacqueline Bouvier saw each other frequently over the next two years. During that time, she would interview the newly elected senator for her "Inquiring Camera Girl" newspaper column. In June 1953, upon her return from Europe, where she had covered the coronation of Queen Elizabeth II for the *Washington Times-Herald,* Jacqueline Bouvier accepted John Kennedy's proposal of marriage.

On the morning of September 12, 1953, more than 750 guests filled St. Mary's Church in Newport, Rhode Island, to watch as John Kennedy and Jacqueline Bouvier exchanged wedding vows. For the occasion, the church had been decorated with pink gladiolus and white chrysanthemums. Boston tenor Luigi Vena sang "Ave Maria." Following the forty-minute ceremony, at which a papal blessing was read, the new couple emerged into a throng of three thousand well-wishers as they made their way with a motorcycle escort to Hammersmith Farm, the Auchincloss estate overlooking Narragansett Bay.

Late in the afternoon, Senator and Mrs. Kennedy departed Hammersmith Farm amid a shower of paper rose petals. They traveled to New York to spend their first night together at the Waldorf-Astoria before continuing on to Acapulco, Mexico, for a public two-week honeymoon.

But their real honeymoon happened right after that, at the secluded San Ysidro Ranch in San Ysidro, California, near Santa Barbara. Spanish for "Saint Isidore," San Ysidro traces its history back to 1769, when King Carlos III of Spain decreed the land to be colonized by Catholic missionaries. In 1825 the former mission was bought by Tomas Olivera, who built an adobe cottage for his wife, which is still standing today. Nestled in the foothills, the five-hundred-acre ranch overlooks the Pacific Ocean and the Channel Islands.

There are no signs marking the cottage where the Kennedys stayed, but the staff knows which one it is. Just ask for the J&J room.

Chelsea Hotel, Room 100, New York City

> The Chelsea has always been a sort of Tower of Babel of creativity and bad behavior. Some of the world's most gifted and most destructive minds have called 222 West 23rd Street home.
>
> *—International Herald Tribune*

Built in 1900 as an apartment building and converted into a hotel in 1905, the Chelsea became a favorite of musicians and artists. Some of the famous guests even paid their rent in paintings and sculptures, which adorn the hotel. The guest list over the years included Jack Kerouac, Arthur Miller, Sam Shepard, Tennessee Williams, Edith Piaf, Henri Cartier-Bresson, Leonard Cohen, Willem de Kooning, Jane Fonda, Janis Joplin, Milos Forman, Jimi Hendrix, Dennis Hopper, Robert Mapplethorpe, and Patti Smith.

But the story of Sid and Nancy that took place there is that of a modern-day Romeo and Juliet. Sid Vicious, born John Simon Ritchie, was the bass player in one of the most controversial punk bands ever, the Sex Pistols. He replaced original bassist Glen Matlock, whom the band had sacked. Nancy Spungen was both a groupie and a junkie. She met Sid at a friend's house, where the two became enamored of each other. Together they slowly began their drug-fueled downward spiral. Band member Johnny Rotten (John Lydon), fed up with Sid's inaccessibility, announced the band's breakup after a fourteen-day U.S. tour.

Sid and Nancy then flew to Paris and worked on the documentary *The Great Rock and Roll Swindle*. Eventually they moved to New York, where Nancy urged him to pursue a solo career. In New York, a depressed and drugged-out Nancy begged Sid to end her life. He refused initially, though later he carried out her wishes. On October 11, 1978, she was found in room 100 of the Chelsea Hotel with a knife in her belly, and Sid was charged with murder.

Several months later Sid was released on bail. He moved in with his mother and wrote letters to Nancy. Not long after, Sid was found dead from a heroin overdose. It's unknown whether it was suicide or an accident. After his cremation, his mom climbed the wall of the cemetery where Nancy is buried and sprinkled his ashes over her grave.

If room 100 isn't your style, then ask for room 211. In 1965 Bob Dylan moved in with his wife, Sara, and worked on his album *Blonde on Blonde* there.

Ritz-Carlton, Suite 534, Sydney, Australia

On November 22, 1997, Michael Hutchence, the lead singer of the popular Australian rock group INXS, was found dead in his suite, number 534, at the Ritz-Carlton, Double Bay, Sydney, Australia. Shortly after noon, the maid found his body, after Hutchence had hanged himself using his own belt. Also found in the room were five different kinds of medication, including the antidepressant Prozac. INXS was in town to kick off their twentieth-anniversary tour. Although the hotel is no longer a Ritz-Carlton, the room is still available in the Sir Stamford Hotel at Double Bay.

Chateau Marmont, Bungalow #2, Hollywood, California

Pudgy and manic, John Belushi was hugely popular in the late 1970s when he starred on TV's *Saturday Night Live* and played the crass Bluto Blutarski in the campus comedy *Animal House* (1978). Belushi won an Emmy Award for *Saturday Night Live,* where his characters included a crazed samurai and a comical killer bee. His longtime creative partnership with his friend Dan Aykroyd included the 1980 movie *The Blues Brothers* and Steven Spielberg's 1979 war comedy, *1941.*

In March 1982, Belushi was found dead in a Beverly Hills hotel bungalow from a drug overdose. He was only thirty-three when he died. The night before he was found, he had visited the Roxy nightclub with Robert De Niro and Robin Williams. The coroner ruled the cause of death to be an accidental overdose of cocaine and heroin, a combination sometimes called a "speedball." An acquaintance of Belushi's, Cathy Smith, was later sentenced to a short prison term for supplying Belushi with the drugs.

Lizzie Borden Bed and Breakfast, Fall River, Massachusetts

> Lizzie Borden took an axe,
> Gave her mother 40 whacks.
> When she saw what she had done,
> Gave her father 41.

One of the most famous unsolved crimes in American history happened in Fall River, Massachusetts. Now you can stay in the room where Abby Borden was killed with an ax and you can visit in the parlor where Andrew J. Borden was found butchered on August 4, 1892.

The Victorian homestead where Abby and Andrew Borden were killed over a century ago is now the Lizzie Borden Bed and Breakfast, after spending most of its life as a private residence. An antique clock ticks away the seconds in the room where Andrew Borden was killed. The Victorian sofa on which he sat when he was whacked is gone, replaced by a replica. In fact, none of the original furniture remains. Nonetheless, people come to see the house, and they can stay in the upstairs room where Abby Borden was killed.

The combination bed-and-breakfast and museum is named after Andrew J. Borden's youngest daughter, Lizzie. Although she was tried and acquitted of the crimes, Lizzie was ostracized by the community of Fall River, many of whom still considered her to be guilty.

Regency Hotel, Room 1831, New York City

Breaking up is hard; breaking up a hotel room, however, is easy. In June 1991, while he was in New York to host *Saturday Night Live*, Kiefer Sutherland and Julia Roberts, then a very hot item, broke up. Somehow the news leaked, and Sutherland heard about the leak when he returned to the Regency Hotel.

A few hours later, he called the hotel's general manager and asked if he could meet with him in the lobby bar in ten minutes. When the GM showed, Sutherland greeted him with three words: "I'm so sorry."

He had totally trashed his room, number 1831, in response to the news of the breakup becoming public. Anything not bolted down was either fractured, splintered, broken, or damaged beyond repair.

Sutherland continued to apologize as hotel staffers totaled up the damage. And then he promptly paid for it.

Mark Hotel, Room 1410, New York City

A number of other guests heard loud noises and banging coming from room 1410, the top suite in New York's upscale Mark Hotel, in the late evening and early morning hours of September 13, 1994. Security was summoned to the fourteenth floor, and when no one responded to their knocks on the door, they opened it. Inside, they found actor Johnny Depp and a $2,000-a-night room that had been totally trashed. Hiding in the closet was his girlfriend at the time, model Kate Moss.

Police arrived at the 77th Street address, went upstairs, and arrested Depp. Charges were later dismissed after Depp spent several hours in a police precinct holding cell and his business manager messengered a check for $9,767.12 in damages.

Ironically, musician Roger Daltry of the Who, a band notorious for trashing hotel rooms, was in the room next door—number 1414—and slept through the entire incident.

Treetops Lodge, Africa

In 1952, Princess Elizabeth of England was on her honeymoon with Prince Philip. While staying at the only suite at the Treetops Lodge in Africa she learned that her father, King George VI, had died, resulting in her subsequent accession to the British throne. Legend has it that she entered the Treetops a princess and left a queen. A stamp was even issued to commemorate the occasion.

The Lodge and Spa at Cordillera, Suite 35, Edwards, Colorado

Suite 35 at the Lodge and Spa at Cordillera, in Edwards, Colorado, is a room that Los Angeles Lakers star Kobe Bryant would love to forget. On June 30, 2003, Bryant, who was traveling with three bodyguards, checked in to have outpatient knee surgery at a nearby clinic. Bryant or one of his bodyguards summoned a hotel employee to his room that evening. That employee was a nineteen-year-old woman. Accounts vary, but sometime between twenty minutes and two hours later the woman returned to the lobby, visibly shaken. During that time Bryant and the unnamed woman had had sexual relations. Whether it was consensual or constituted an assault was up to the jury to decide.

Milford Plaza Hotel, Room 603, New York City

On October 5, 2002, three sailors were on weekend leave from their ship, the U.S.S. *Wasp*, at its berth in Earle, New Jersey. The sailors were Naval Petty Officer Brian Cooley, age twenty-nine, of LaPorte, Indiana, Lisa Tedstone, age thirty, of Simpsonville, South Carolina, and Jeremy Worrell, age twenty-five, of Virginia. During an evening of bar hopping in New York, Tedstone refused Cooley's sexual advances. At the same time, the group decided against returning to the ship and rented a room at the Milford Plaza, on West 45th Street. Apparently, Tedstone then climbed into bed with the passed-out Worrell, a strictly platonic move. This infuriated Cooley, who left to get his own room.

Shortly after 3 A.M. Cooley returned to the room, using his key, and started an argument with Tedstone. According to the criminal complaint, Worrell told police Cooley "grabbed Tedstone by the arm, punched her twice about the body, and forcibly shoved her in the direction of the open window, while she was yelling, 'No, stop it.'"

Worrell then said he saw Tedstone "go out the open window," and Cooley left the room. Both men just went back to sleep, leaving Tedstone lying on 8th Avenue. Lisa Tedstone had fallen six floors to her death—not exactly Cinderella Liberty.

Oasis Motel, Room 20, Las Vegas, Nevada

On March 22, 1998, at 10:30 A.M., the Oasis Motel front desk clerk called room 20 to remind the guest, David Strickland, an actor then appearing on the TV show *Suddenly Susan*, that checkout time was 11:00 A.M. When she did not get an answer, she took the master key, went to room 20, knocked on the door, and opened it with the master key. She found David Strickland's body hanging by a king-size sheet from the wooden beams in the ceiling, a chair behind him.

Regency Hotel, Room 725, New York City

Sometimes guests break up the room simply because it's there.

Comedian Sam Kinison was legendary for the condition in which he left his hotel rooms. And room 725 at the Regency in

New York was no exception. In early 1992, he was in New York doing a movie that apparently was so bad it could be neither finished nor released. He returned to the room, closed the door, and became a one-man wrecking crew. Pictures, chairs, lamps, desks, even bathroom fixtures were ripped from the walls. By the time hotel security responded to other guest complaints about the excessive noise, there wasn't much left standing in the room. To make matters worse, the toilet was backed up with drug paraphernalia Kinison had tried to flush when the authorities arrived.

He paid for the damage to the room. A few weeks later, in April 1992, the thirty-eight-year-old Kinison died in a car crash on a desert road between Los Angeles and Las Vegas.

Regency Hotel, Room 901, New York City

Room 901 at the Regency Hotel was where it was supposed to happen. Frank Gifford was cheating on his wife, Kathie Lee, and arranged a rendezvous with a busty flight attendant, who was also cheating on her husband. The flight attendant was paid $50,000 by a tabloid newspaper to trap Gifford in the act. The newspaper hired a TV crew to catch the action on tape. But what no one knew was that the husband of the flight attendant wanted to catch *her* in the act, and he also hired a TV crew. While Gifford and the flight attendant were kissing in the room, fights broke out in the hallway and on the balcony as the two competing television crews battled it out for prime viewing position.

Canterbury Hotel, Room 606, Indianapolis, Indiana

Mike Tyson was sentenced to ten years in prison for the rape of Desiree Washington, an eighteen-year-old college student. She was a contestant in the Miss Black America Pageant, which Tyson attended in July 1991 at the invitation of Reverend Charles Williams. Washington accepted a late-night date with

Tyson and says he raped her in his hotel room, then laughed about it as she wept.

Tyson told the judge at his sentencing, "I don't come here begging for mercy, ma'am. I can't see anything good coming from this. I'm here prepared for the worst. I've been crucified, humiliated worldwide." Tyson further said that "when I came to Indiana my conduct was kind of crass . . . [but] I have not raped anyone, tried to rape anyone by any means. I'm sorry for Miss Washington as a person. I by no means meant to hurt her or do anything to her. I'm sure she knows that."

Washington has said, "In the place of what has been me for eighteen years is now a cold and empty feeling. I am not able to comment on what my future will be, I can only say that each day after being raped has been a struggle to learn to trust again, to smile the way I did and to find the Desiree Washington who was stolen from me and from those who love me on July 19, 1991."

St. Francis Hotel, Room 1221, San Francisco, California

In 1921 Roscoe "Fatty" Arbuckle was one of the highest-paid actor/directors in the motion picture business. But on September 5 of that year, during a weekend party he was throwing at the St. Francis Hotel in San Francisco, his life turned a corner. Virginia Rappe, a girl attending the party, ran screaming from a bedroom, took sick, and died four days later.

On September 17, Roscoe Arbuckle was arraigned in San Francisco, charged with the rape and murder of Virginia Rappe. The legendary producer Adolph Zukor (who footed the legal bill) tried to bring in the great trial lawyer Earl Rogers, but Rogers was in ill health and couldn't take the case. Rogers spoke prophetically of Fatty's plight: "They will make it very tough on him, because of his weight. A man of that enormous fatness being charged with the rape of a young girl will prejudice them, even just the thought of it."

Arbuckle's wife stuck by him throughout the trial—such was the public's scorn that she was shot at while entering the courthouse—but the producers in Hollywood forbade Arbuckle's movie friends to testify on his behalf, fearing that their careers would be besmirched and that the scandal would cut into profits.

The ugliest twist—one many people are unaware of—is that Arbuckle was completely innocent. He was set up by a woman named Maude Delmont, known as "Madame Black." Delmont would provide girls for parties and then have the girl claim she was raped by a prominent director or producer. Concerned about his career, the victim would submit to Delmont's request for money to keep the story out of the press. When Rappe died a few days after the party, from a condition unrelated to the events at the St. Francis Hotel, Delmont gave Fatty Arbuckle's name to the police.

After two trials resulted in hung juries, Fatty was acquitted at the third, with a written apology from the jury.

It was, of course, too little too late. Will Hays, the former postmaster general, had been installed as a kind of overlord-pope charged with cleaning up the movies for America. As Arbuckle faced his second trial, "Hays went into a sort of metaphorical desert to consult with his conscience. . . . On April 19, 1922, Will Hays made the first major policy decision of his new job. He banned Roscoe Arbuckle from the screen." Arbuckle died a few years later. But the hotel room lives on.

OTHER HOTEL ROOM ARRESTS

Vista International Hotel, Room 511, Washington, D.C.

Washington, D.C., Mayor Marion Barry was arrested on charges of possession of cocaine on January 18, 1990, in room 511 at the Vista International Hotel after a fast-moving undercover investigation by the FBI and D.C. police. This room is notorious for the mayor's famous quote, "The bitch set me up," when he was busted.

The mayor, arrested on narcotics charges shortly after 8 P.M., had smoked crack cocaine in the hotel room. He was with a longtime female friend, who did not smoke cocaine or engage in sexual activity with the mayor before his arrest. The encounter took place over the course of about an hour and was both video-taped and audiotaped by the FBI.

Thomas E. DuHadway, who headed the Washington FBI field office, said of the sting, "The undercover operation was part of an ongoing public corruption probe under the supervision of the U.S. Attorney for the District of Columbia." The operation had begun several weeks earlier, just as a yearlong grand jury investigation into allegations that the mayor had used crack cocaine with Charles Lewis, a former D.C. employee and convicted cocaine dealer, appeared to be drawing to a close.

Barry had steadfastly denied using drugs since allegations had first surfaced against him in 1981, and he was expected to announce his campaign for a fourth term on the following Sunday.

Barry was convicted and served a sentence for crack cocaine possession. After his release, he was reelected mayor. The hotel is now the Wyndham, but the room is still rented regularly to guests who ask for it.

Bentley Hotel, South Beach, California

Dennis Rodman and his wife at the time, actress Carmen Electra, were arrested following reports that they fought after a night of partying in South Beach.

Officers were called to the Bentley Hotel in South Beach at 7 A.M., following a disturbance. Police had received calls complaining of people fighting and loud noises. Rodman's shirt was torn, and the room was in disarray when officers arrived. Electra had a bruise on her arm, an injury to her left temple, and a swollen lip from Rodman allegedly throwing her purse at her face. She also cut a toe on her left foot after being thrown outside their hotel room, the police report said. Both Rodman and Electra left the hotel in handcuffs.

While in custody, Rodman, a seven-time NBA rebounding champion who has played for the Chicago Bulls, San Antonio Spurs, and Detroit Pistons, asked authorities to tell Electra that he was sorry he had overreacted and that he loved her, the police report said.

Rodman and Electra had been married on November 14, 1998, in Las Vegas. Nine days after their wedding, Rodman announced he was seeking an annulment, claiming he had been of unsound mind when he recited his vows. But he never received an annulment, and by February the pair were again appearing together publicly, holding a news conference at the opening of a Beverly Hills, California, restaurant. During that news conference, Rodman said that he and his wife were happily married but were living in separate homes. She later attended several Los Angeles Lakers games to watch her husband play. On March 13, Rodman received permission to leave the Lakers to resolve personal issues and returned to the team about two weeks later. The team released him before the season ended that April.

On the night in question, Rodman and Electra were charged with simple battery, and both spent several hours in custody.

Sheraton Plaza La Reina Hotel, Suite 587, Los Angeles Airport

On October 18, 1982, automaker John DeLorean held a meeting in suite 587 at the Sheraton Plaza La Reina Hotel at the Los Angeles Airport to broker a cocaine deal in an attempt to save his failing car company. DeLorean was shown a suitcase containing twenty kilograms of cocaine and was told by a DEA agent he could expect to receive $5 million from the sale. DeLorean stated that it was "in the nick of time," since the British government had announced that October 22, 1982, would be the last day of operation for his plant in Ireland. The entire meeting was caught on the DEA's videotape—FBI pinhole camera footage taken through the wall of the room next door—and DeLorean was arrested.

Merv Griffin's Givenchy Resort, Room 311, Palm Springs, California

In 1987, after it was revealed that television evangelist Jim Bakker had had numerous hotel room sexual encounters with church secretary Jessica Hahn, the Sheraton in Clearwater Florida was inundated with requests to rent the Bakker room. "It sells so good," said Russ Kimball, the hotel's general manager, "I'm thinking about putting '538' on every room on the fifth floor." And thirteen years later, at a hotel in California, Merv Griffin had the same idea.

On November 25, 2000, police received a 911 call from an anonymous male source who claimed there was a man with cocaine and guns in the hotel room where Robert Downey Jr. was staying at Merv Griffin's resort hotel. A tape of the call stated: "Uh yeah, I'd just like to let you know that in room 311 at the Merv Griffin Resort there's a man that has an ounce of cocaine and a couple of guns and is pretty upset. Thank you." Downey was picked up at about 9:45 P.M. at the posh, celeb-friendly resort in the southern California desert community. Police said they arrived at the hotel and Downey agreed to let them in. They found no weapons, but they did find a white powder in a brown prescription-pill bottle, later determined to be 4.5 grams of methamphetamine and cocaine.

"He was very cooperative through the investigation and did not offer any resistance. But he did show signs of being under the influence of a central nervous system stimulant," Palm Springs police sergeant Don Craiger told the *Desert Sun* newspaper.

This arrest came just three months after Downey was freed

from prison, where he had served a year for a previous drug conviction. He was released when an appeals court ruled that there had been a sentencing error in his case.

While in custody, Downey reportedly asked arresting officer Brian Anderson for a cigarette. Anderson declined Downey's request, saying he didn't want to give him special celebrity treatment, to which Downey reportedly responded, "I'm not a movie star right now. I'm just a guy with a drug problem."

One of the funniest responses to the arrest of Downey came from hotel owner Merv Griffin. So many people began calling the hotel and asking for room 311 that Griffin ordered his general manager to change ten of the room numbers to 311! The hotel was recently sold to the owner of Le Parker Meridien Hotel in Manhattan. And the hotel is now back down to just a single room 311.

HISTORY HAPPENED HERE

Here are some other hotel rooms where history was made.

Manila Hotel, Room 901, Philippines

Many noted historic visitors have graced this room, including Britain's Prince Charles, pop star Michael Jackson, and General Douglas MacArthur. MacArthur, famous for his promise, "I shall return," made the Manila Hotel his residence and headquarters from 1935 to 1941. The mere mention of the general's name would bring warm tears of memory and affection to the eyes of those who worked there during those years. MacArthur, the hotel's most famous resident, was then and is now a hero to the Filipinos who knew and served him.

Sent to the Philippines at the outbreak of the Spanish-American War, after Admiral Dewey's defeat of the Spanish naval forces in Manila Bay, MacArthur's father, General Arthur

MacArthur, was given the job of heading the combined U.S. and Filipino ground forces in order to drive the Spaniards out of Manila. Under the treaty of peace with Spain that followed, the Philippines was ceded to the United States by Spain, upon payment of $29 million, and General Arthur MacArthur became the islands' first American military governor.

In 1935 President Quezon asked Douglas MacArthur, when his tour of duty as chief of staff ended, to come to the Philippines as his military adviser. MacArthur agreed. Among the terms of their agreement, they discussed fitting living quarters for the American general—something that would be comparable to those now occupied by the American governor-general in Manila, at Malacanang Palace. MacArthur's personal palace in Manila was to be the penthouse built especially for him atop the Manila Hotel.

Hotel Theresa, Room 18, Harlem

Cuba's Fidel Castro has great fondness for New York's Harlem and for black Americans in general, having visited the neighborhood during a 1960 trip to the United Nations. Refused at the Shelbourne Hotel in midtown at that time, the delegation of bearded guerrillas, who had recently assumed power in Cuba, moved to Harlem's Hotel Theresa. Thousands of Harlem residents crowded the streets to cheer them. While there, Castro plucked his own chickens. He met with black leader Malcolm X and met separately with Soviet leader Nikita Khrushchev.

Castro said of his experience there, "From the time our delegation began traveling through Harlem, from the instant a Black person saw us, he began to wave to us in greeting. In the very heart of the empire there are 20 million Black people, oppressed and exploited. Their aspirations cannot be satisfied with a fistful of dollars, it is a very much more difficult problem, because their aspirations can only be satisfied by justice."

Algonquin Hotel, Room 204, New York City

There isn't a place in New York more important to Dorothy Parker's enduring legacy than the Algonquin Hotel. The "Gonk" is where the notorious Round Table met from 1919 to 1929. They were the most celebrated literary group ever to gather in American letters. It was here that Parker wrote part of the script for the film *A Star Is Born*, and it is where Harold Ross created *The New Yorker* magazine.

The hotel was the home base for the group for ten years, as they ruled the New York literati landscape during Prohibition. They would meet here in the Rose Room for long, liquid lunches. Some nights, there would be a poker game upstairs in one of their rooms. During this period, Parker was in her midtwenties and early thirties. She wrote "Ballad at 35" in August 1928, at the height of the Round Table's popularity. This was the most industrious period of her life.

After Parker split from her husband, Eddie, for a second time in 1924, she moved into a furnished suite on the second floor at the Algonquin.

After the Round Table disbanded, Parker returned to the hotel in 1932, when she made one of her many suicide attempts, this time with sleeping pills.

HOTELS AND MOVIES

Hotels have featured prominently in many major movies. Here are a few of the most famous.

Grand Hotel des Bains, Venice, Italy
Death in Venice

This hotel was the setting for Thomas Mann's turn-of-the-century novel as well as the film based on it, which won the Grand Prix award at the 1971 Cannes Film Festival. The film was directed by Luchino Visconti.

Ritz, London, England
Notting Hill

Movie Director Roger Mitchell chose the Trafalgar Suite for the scene where Hugh Grant posed as a journalist from an equestrian magazine to interview Julia Roberts. The Ritz is prominently featured throughout the movie, from the front desk, where Hugh Grant tries to decipher Julia Roberts's alias using Disney characters' names, to the Piccadilly Arcade.

The Columns, New Orleans, Louisiana
Pretty Baby

A Victorian mansion built by a tobacco merchant in 1883 served as the backdrop for Louis Malles's controversial film *Pretty Baby*, starring Brooke Shields. The film is set in 1917 in a brothel in the New Orleans Garden District. The romantic interiors of the hotel, from the mahogany staircase and stained glass window to the antique-filled rooms, evoke a moment from the movie.

Carlton Intercontinental, Cannes, France
To Catch a Thief

The Belle Époque façade of the grand Carlton Hotel was the setting for Alfred Hitchcock's 1955 film *To Catch a Thief*, starring Grace Kelly and Cary Grant. This was one of the first Hollywood motion pictures to be shot on location. The entire crew stayed at the hotel while filming, which enabled Kelly to go to Monaco and meet Prince Rainier. From the first moment of the film, on the hotel balcony overlooking the Mediterranean, to Grace Kelly's first kiss with Cary Grant in front of her room (number 541), the Carlton and the Riviera are magnificently portrayed throughout the movie.

Hotel del Coronado, San Diego, California
Some Like It Hot

Billy Wilder's and David O. Selznick's 1958 black-and-white comedy classic starred Marilyn Monroe, Jack Lemmon, and

Tony Curtis. This 1888 Victorian chef-d'oeuvre hotel is the perfect setting for this Prohibition-era film about two men who join an all-woman band to escape from gangsters. In both the beach scenes and those in the nightclub, you will immediately recognize this legendary hotel.

Regent Beverly Wilshire, Los Angeles, California
Pretty Woman

The Regent Beverly Wilshire has been filmed for movies more than almost any other hotel. It is most famous for its 1990 debut in Gary Marshall's *Pretty Woman*, starring Julia Roberts and Richard Gere. In the movie the couple stayed in the Presidential Suite, which was partially reconstructed in the studio.

The hotel was also the posh setting for Eddie Murphy's character, Axel Foley, in *Beverly Hills Cop* and was the backdrop for Quentin Tarantino's film *True Romance*.

Famous residents of this hotel have included Warren Beatty, who lived in the Veranda Suite for years. In the 1950s Elvis lived here for several years while making a movie at nearby Paramount Studios. And because Elvis had lived there, John Lennon chose the hotel as his residence while estranged from Yoko Ono for several months. Dashiell Hammett wrote *The Thin Man* while living here.

Honorable Mentions

- Grand Hotel, Mackinac Island, Michigan: *Somewhere in Time*, starring Jane Seymour and Christopher Reeves, was filmed here.

- Los Angeles Bonaventure: *True Lies*, starring Arnold Schwarzenegger, featured this hotel.

- Palms Hotel and Casino, Las Vegas: The MTV Real World Suite is located here. The hotel took six standard rooms and did a million-dollar makeover to create a 2,900-square-foot supersuite with a whirlpool, a pool table, a three-hundred-gallon aquarium, and a view of the strip.

CELEBRITY ROOMS

Hotel Pera Palace, Room 411, Istanbul, Turkey

In 1926, Agatha Christie disappeared for eleven days while writing *Murder on the Orient Express* in room 411. She later claimed to remember nothing, and it's a mystery that is still unsolved. In 1976, Warner Brothers tried to make a movie about her disappearance and summoned a famous psychic to unlock the mystery. Agatha Christie's spirit dictated a message to her: "The key to the mystery of my disappearance can be found at the Pera Palace in Istanbul." And indeed a key was found underneath the wooden boards in the spot she indicated. What the key unlocks remains a mystery to this day.

Beverly Hills Hotel, Bungalows 20 and 21, Los Angeles, California

The "Pink Palace" has become legendary in Hollywood. Its bar, the Polo Lounge, would boast, "It attracts more stars than the sky"—the same motto used by MGM.

Owned by the sultan of Brunei, the Pink Palace has been guarding the secrets of Hollywood's rich and famous for over ninety years. The twenty-two bungalows have provided the perfect cover for some of Hollywood royalty's less public engagements. Carole Lombard and Clark Gable, Katharine Hepburn and Spencer Tracy—just about every famous Hollywood couple who cheated on their spouses did it here. Even investment banker Ivan Boesky lured financier Michael Milken to his suite at the Beverly Hills Hotel, where their conversation was recorded by the FBI and led to charges of insider trading.

In 1960, while filming *Let's Make Love*, Yves Montand and

Simone Signoret shared an apartment identical to that of Marilyn Monroe and Arthur Miller in the same bungalow, separated by a common lobby, at numbers 20 and 21. Shortly thereafter, the on-screen romance began to spill into everyday life and the newspapers, as Montand and Monroe simply slipped next door. At the end of shooting, Montand returned to France.

Plaza Hotel, Suite 437 and the Plaza Grand Ballroom, New York

Truman Capote was the host of the famous Black and White Dance in the Plaza Grand Ballroom on November 28, 1966. Everyone who was anyone fought to get an invitation. The guest list included Frank Sinatra, Mia Farrow, Candice Bergen, Mr. and Mrs. Leonard Bernstein, Noel Coward, Oscar de la Renta, Greta Garbo, Mr. and Mrs. Henry Fonda, the maharajah of Jaipur, Mrs. Joseph Kennedy, Prince Amyn Khan, Vivien Leigh, Lauren Bacall, and Andy Warhol, as well as various other senators, movie moguls, and actors and actresses.

Ambos Mundos, Room 511, Havana, Cuba

In the early 1930s Ernest Hemingway left Key West for Old Havana and checked into Room 511 of the Ambos Mundos Hotel, where he wrote *For Whom the Bell Tolls*. He worked every day from 8 A.M. to 2 P.M., then he would sail on his yacht with his quartermaster Gregorio Fuentes, who was his inspiration for the title character in *The Old Man and the Sea*. Ambos Mundos was his base in Cuba for seven years; he always checked into room 511, paying $2 per day. Room 511 has been kept much the same way since he left, with his typewriter under glass on the desk on which he worked. Hemingway remarked of the place, "Ambos Mundos is a good place for writing."

Meurice, Presidential Suite, Rooms 106–108, Paris, France

For two months each year for thirty years Salvador Dali stayed in rooms 106–108 on the first floor of the Meurice in Paris, starting with his first trip to Paris in 1927. Known for his eccentric flair, the surrealist artist would give interviews and entertain in his suite or just sit in a salon in the foyer to read.

Peninsula, Suites 505 and 506 and Suites 305 and 306, Hong Kong

In 1962, Frank Sinatra embarked on a world concert tour. On April 28 of that year, he arrived at the Peninsula with an entourage of twenty people, including his musicians, friends, photographer, three TV cameramen, and two public relations executives. That entourage followed him everywhere. His suites, numbers 505 and 506, had spectacular views of the harbor. Because he was trying to win goodwill, he was always handing out $50 tips to the staff. Sinatra returned three more times to the Peninsula (to rooms 305 and 306).

Goldeneye, Jamaica

Ian Fleming bought land in Jamaica in 1944 and built a simple, U-shaped villa. Over the twenty-year period during which he visited, Goldeneye slowly evolved into a luxurious hideaway. Since then, the property has become the Goldeneye Resort. Inspired by his surroundings, this is where Fleming started writing the James Bond novels—his desk is still in the bedroom. *Dr. No*, the first James Bond movie, was filmed at Goldeneye. Ian Fleming's Jamaican retreat is available for rent as a private villa or you can rent the entire property.

Hotel D'Angleterre, Danny Kaye Suite, Copenhagen, Denmark

The Danish capital's Hotel D'Angleterre decided to name a hotel suite for Danny Kaye after his performance as the title character in the 1952 movie *Hans Christian Andersen*. When the actor strolled cobblestone streets while singing "Wonderful Copenhagen" he earned the love of the nation and made the song a part of Danish national identity.

The third-floor, two-room suite features views of the historic King Square, the Royal Danish Opera House, and the Nyhavn Canal. Framed photos of Kaye adorn the walls.

Hotel Lancaster, Marlene Dietrich Suite, Paris, France

The Hotel Lancaster was the Parisian home of film legend Marlene Dietrich for more than three years in the 1930s. The suite's current décor is an homage to Dietrich, furnished in her favorite shades of purple and lilac. Her portrait, drawn by her mentor and one-time paramour, Josef von Sternberg, hangs above the bed, a reminder of Dietrich's faded beauty.

Chateau du Sureau, Elderberry Room, Oakhurst, California

Barbra Streisand has stayed here.

Amangani, Teton Suite, Jackson Hole, Wyoming

Sandra Bullock has stayed here.

Taos Inn, Suite 105, Taos, New Mexico

Robert Redford, Julia Roberts, and Keanu Reeves have all stayed here—separately, of course.

Hotel Parisi, La Jolla Suite, La Jolla, California

Madonna has stayed here.

Gastonian, Garden Suite, Savannah, Georgia

Ben Affleck has stayed here, which perhaps gave him the idea to later buy an estate in the area.

Cibolo Creek Ranch, Shafter, Texas

What do Mick Jagger and Dan Rather have in common? They've both stayed in the Fort La Morita cabin.

Woodlands Resort & Inn, Room 103, Summerville, South Carolina

Actor Bruce Willis stays here when he is in the area.

FAMOUS BEDS

Washington may actually have slept in some of these beds—and now you can, too.

Eisenhower Apartment, Culzean Castle, Maybole, Ayrshire, Scotland

Culzean Castle came to the National Trust in 1945 when the Kennedy family who owned it was forced to sell it to pay back debts. The family sold the property on one condition: that the top floor be kept as a private apartment for General Dwight D. Eisenhower, as a thank-you for his courageous leadership of Scottish forces during Word War II. Eisenhower visited the castle four times, including once during his presidency in 1959. Present-day visitors can look back to the first page of the registry and find Eisenhower's entry, dated 1945.

The Eisenhower Apartment is billed as the "most exclusive accommodation in Scotland." The apartment has six bedrooms, a dining room, a drawing room, and an oval, pillared staircase. The walls of the apartment are decorated with Eisenhower-related treasured mementos, family photos, letters, and trinkets from the White House. Prince Charles and Sean Connery have also stayed in this apartment.

THE MOST-BOMBED HOTEL: At the latest count, the Europa Hotel in Belfast, Ireland, had been bombed thirty-three times between 1970 and 1995, giving it the singular and undisputedly dubious distinction of being the most-bombed hotel in the world.

Home for journalists covering the years of "troubles" in northern Ireland, the Europa, although it was certainly a target, was also the source of intensely black humor and is now looked back on with a sort of demented fondness.

There was the time in 1971 when two young gunmen calmly walked into the reception lobby and deposited a large white box marked "IRA"—stuffed full of explosives—beside the elevators. "Don't move until this goes off," one of the gunmen told staff and guests.

Then there was the occasion when the hall porter noticed a furniture van parked outside and was expecting it to blow up. He was approached by an American guest who demanded he be given a letter from the hotel's room mailboxes located behind the front desk. "You'll be getting it by airmail shortly," the porter said, with an eye on the van.

One day the Europa's legendary first general manager, Harper Brown, watched members of the IRA enter the lobby with a bomb in a box. Mr. Brown picked it up and took it out to the parking lot. The IRA saw him, and in turn, as in some terrible farce, brought it back in again. The redoubtable Mr. Brown carried it straight back out, at which point the IRA gave up and left.

No matter what happened, the hotel never closed, even when it was very badly damaged, and today you're more than likely to find some IRA veterans at the hotel bar, boxless, but with drinks in hand, ready to tell the stories.

Thomas Jefferson Inn at Meander Plantation, Locust Dale, Virginia

As a friend of the family who owned it, Thomas Jefferson slept here when it was a private home.

Old Tavern at Grafton, Grafton, Vermont

One of the oldest active inns in New England, the Old Tavern first opened in 1801. Ulysses S. Grant, Daniel Webster, Oliver Wendell Holmes, Nathaniel Hawthorne, Ralph Waldo Emerson, Rudyard Kipling, and Henry David Thoreau have all stayed here.

Cuthbert House, Beaufort, South Carolina

In 1861 during his march through the Confederacy, General William T. Sherman stayed at this home when it was used for Union (Yankee) soldiers.

CHAPTER 13

Additional Resources

HOTEL FREQUENT-STAY PROGRAMS

A lot has been written about airline frequent-flyer programs, and this much is clear: these are loyalty programs that have gotten out of hand—and more often than not, they fail to reward travelers for their loyalty, unless these frequent flyers are intent on taking a trip to Des Moines on a Wednesday in February at two in the afternoon.

These airline programs are wildly profitable for the airlines: first, because they have hundreds of marketing partners, to whom they sell miles at the rate of between 2 and $2\frac{1}{2}$¢ per mile, and second, because of the pathetic rates of redemption. Some airlines actually like to boast about how difficult they make it for their mileage members to actually redeem their miles.

The same principles apply to many hotel frequent-stay programs, although the situation with hotels can actually be worse. For example, if I earn all my miles by flying to Cleveland but want to redeem them for a free flight to San Francisco, assuming the miles are actually redeemed and the airline actually flies me there, no one within the airline complains.

Hotels are structured differently, however, and at the chain level you are dealing with multiple and different owners. Using the same scenario, if I earned all my frequent-stay points at a Marriott in Cleveland but wanted to redeem them at a Marriott in San Francisco, there might be some problems. Why? Because the hotels have different owners and the San Francisco hotel would presumably be the more popular hotel for redemption rather than accrual of points.

When Marriott started its frequent-stay program, hotel executives recognized this disparity and attempted to deal with it by establishing a centralized separate fund. If you stayed at that

Marriott in Cleveland and asked for points to be credited to your Marriott account, then about 7 percent of your entire bill was contributed to the fund by that hotel. Later, when you went to redeem your points, the hotel honoring those points received a negotiated room rate in dollars from that fund. And that, essentially, is how most hotel frequent-stay programs work.

That didn't stop some companies, including Marriott, from imposing blackout periods during peak seasons—to keep individual hotel owners happy. After all, why would a hotel owner be excited to redeem points at a negotiated rate of $150 per night in Scottsdale in December, when he could fill his hotel at $350 per room per night?

Soon, hotel frequent-stay members were becoming as frustrated as frequent-flyer program members. The folks earning the highest number of points for the most paid stays were being refused when they finally wanted to get that room for a week in Hawaii or Arizona or the Caribbean.

Starwood recognized the inequity of this situation and instituted a commonsense approach to appeasing its hotel owners. The new program basically dedicates a certain amount of room inventory to the program at a negotiated price. However, anytime a hotel exceeds 92 percent occupancy, a higher negotiated rate—sometimes even the full rate—kicks in, and if a room is available and you have the points, you are in. You would be locked out of redeeming your points only in a situation where a hotel was truly sold out. This is a much better way to go—the airlines should follow this Starwood model.

In recent years, hotel programs have grown so large—and the centralized funds have grown along with them—that individual hotel contributions to those centralized funds are now averaging about 3.5 percent. Still, the numbers are staggering. At any given time, about 35 percent of all guests are accruing points.

With the advent of mileage partners and the buying and selling of points and miles, there is currency confusion out there.

What to redeem, how much to redeem, when to redeem, and, yes, what to redeem it for have become much more complicated propositions.

For example, going back to the 2.5¢ a mile equation, if you earn enough points at a hotel for a free airline ticket, you must assume that the hotel corporation had to go out and buy twenty-five thousand miles from the airline. In real dollars, that's $500. As a result, many hotel programs are looking for less expensive redemption options. Recently, a friend redeemed one hundred thousand Hilton points—not for a free airline ticket, but for a Bose stereo system, which wholesales for $300. The Hilton folks were all too happy to get him that stereo because they saved $200 in redemption costs.

Bottom line: in the long run, the stereo system might have been a better deal for the hotel *and* for the guest. So always look for alternative ways to redeem your frequent-stay points for things other than airline tickets. As many programs start mimicking Starwood, you no longer have to think only about the off-season to get that coveted room.

In fact, for the moment at least, I like hotel frequent-stay programs a whole lot better than the airline programs.

ALTERNATIVE LODGING

Here are some places to stay that can be interesting alternatives to a standard hotel room. Some of these may require an adventuresome spirit.

Ranches and Cabins

Near Santa Barbara, California, you'll find one of the more unique lodgings in the state. For $69 a night, Rancho Oso offers cabins that, on the outside, look like old saloons or general stores from the Wild West. The cabins come with one double bed and a set of bunk beds, a refrigerator, and a coffeemaker. A shared bathroom is a short walk away. Those looking to pay even less in a memorable setting can stay in one of the ranch's Conestoga wagons, which come with four army cots, a barbecue pit, and an electrical outlet, and cost just $45 a night.

◆ (805) 683-5686

www.rancho-oso.com

The Jackson Hole dude ranch is a traditional Old West favorite. Whether you travel alone, as a couple, or with the whole family, the dude ranch offers a chance to enjoy relaxing solitude in a beautiful western setting. Dude ranches are usually situated in secluded locations, away from towns and other ranches. Hearty meals are served family style, with all the guests eating together in a large dining room or lodge. Horseback riding is a staple at most dude ranches, as are fishing, hiking, swimming, raft trips, and park tours. Some are real, functioning ranches where guests can join working cowboys, and others are more luxurious.

◆ Jackson Hole Chamber of Commerce

(307) 733-3316

www.jacksonholechamber.com

Dude Ranchers Association

116 dude ranches in U.S. and Canada

(307) 587-2339

www.duderanch.org

Brooks Lake Lodge

(307) 455-2121

www.brookslake.com

The Spotted Horse Ranch

(800) 528-2084 or (307) 733-2097

www.spottedhorseranch.com

The Cullen Ranch deluxe hunting resort near Dallas, Texas, is a two-thousand-acre spread devoted to the sports of hunting and fishing. Prey include bobwhite quail, chukar, pheasant, and mallard duck. There's also a sporting clay course and ponds stocked with oversized black bass.

The facility has received rave reviews for the pampering it gives guests. In addition to the lodgelike rough-hewn furniture, Persian rugs, and deer-antler chandelier, there is a vintage wine cellar and cigar bar. A French-trained chef prepares the excellent cuisine.

◆ (888) 839-4868

www.cullenranch.com

Located in northeastern Washington and sitting 3,200 feet above the historic Okanogan Highlands, the Eden Valley Guest Ranch offers ten new, deluxe, car-accessible mountain cabins built at the edge of the tree line with great sweeping views. Small by design, visitors to the ranch won't see many people while hiking or horseback riding in the adjoining National Forest.

◆ (509) 485-4002

www.edenvalleyranch.net

(360) 725-5069

www.experiencewashington.com

Yurts

An option that is short on pampering but big on value is the circular, high-roofed tent known as a yurt. At Cachuma Lake Reservation Area (about a half hour from downtown Santa Barbara), yurts are perched right off the lake, sleep up to six, and run only $45 to $65 a night. All the yurts are equipped with electricity, bunks, and heaters. You can also camp the old-fashioned way (bring your own tent) for $16 if you prefer.

◆ (805) 686-5054

www.sbparks.org

(805) 686-5050

www.cachuma.com

Tepees

At Skyland Ranch in Washington state, traditional painted teepees, complete with beds and wood fires, are nestled in a valley next to the Snoqualmie National Forest, which provides 250,000 acres of wilderness for riding and hiking.

◆ (206) 695-9446

www.tipitrek.com

Navajo Hogan

Stay in a family-owned hogan about forty-five minutes west of Window Rock, Arizona, the capital of the Navajo nation.

◆ Two White Rocks

P.O. Box 1187

St. Michaels, AZ 86511

(520) 871-4360

www.whereintheworld.co.uk

Bedouin Tents

Al Maha Desert Resort in Dubai, United Arab Emirates, offers twenty-seven luxurious Bedouin tent suites, an oasis in the heart of the desert overlooking the majestic Hajar Mountains. Each suite is richly decorated with local fabrics and artifacts. Riding, archery, falcon hunting, and camel safaris are available.

◆ 971 4 303 4222

www.al-maha.com

Room with a View

Adventurous travelers can now book a hotel room at the Mena House Oberoi, Giza, Egypt, directly adjacent to the Great Pyramid. Room 498 offers guests an up-close chance to count each and every stone in the pyramid.

◆ 20 2 383 3222

www.oberoihotels.com

Pig Sty

In Italian it sounds romantic . . . until you realize that *il Porcile* means "the pig sty." Mud and straw have been cleared out to make way for a simple but charming apartment. It is compact—the whitewashed living room with wood beams has an inbuilt kitchen and sofa bed—but there's a separate shower room and shared use of a swimming pool. A picturesque village is within walking distance, and Siena is twenty minutes away.

◆ 020 7603 7111

www.invitationtotuscany.com, go to Porcile & Gatto

Lighthouses

Staying in any lighthouse is different, but a lighthouse in Croatia, tipped as one of this year's hottest destinations, is truly special. There are eleven of them along the Croatian coast, some on their own private islands. The Plocica Lighthouse has two apartments, one sleeping six and the other sleeping eight.

◆ 385 (0) 1 3013 666

www.adriatica.net

Triton House, in association with Trinity Lighthouse Services, Britain's national lighthouse authority, is rapidly converting its stock of former lightkeepers' cottages into upmarket tourist lodgings. From just three cottages opened about two years ago in Cornwall, the agency now rents twenty-two cottages at eight lighthouses in England and Wales.

The cottages, some as much as 150 years old, housed lightkeepers and their families until automation eliminated their jobs. The cottages are situated at sea, but they're not for everybody. Most are in remote locations, though some are also near golf courses. There is also the matter of no existing night life.

◆ 01 386 701177

www.ruralretreats.co.uk

Signal Box

Don't worry, trains don't run through this stretch of countryside anymore, so the quaint, converted signal box on the edge of Glenbeigh village at the foot of Seefin Mountain in County Kerry, Ireland, is a peaceful spot. It's also within seven miles of a clean, sandy beach, and is close to centers for many activities, from horseback riding to boats for hire. The signal box has a spiral staircase leading from the kitchen to the bedroom/sitting area.

◆ 44 (0) 1823 660126

www.shamrockcottages.co.uk

Floating Hotel

The floating hotel in the rain forest of the Amazon is called the Flotel Orellana. It is a three-deck, 131-foot converted flat-bottom barge made of Ecuadorian mahogany and laurel wood flown into the jungle piece by piece, then painstakingly rebuilt right there on the river. The lower deck features a dining room, crew's quarters, and a noisy generator. The top deck has cabins for up to fifty-six passengers and double and four-berth units. The cabins are small but offer enough drawer and hanger space for the fifteen pounds of baggage you're permitted on board. Each comfortable, bunk-bedded cabin includes a private bath with a shower. However, the most popular part of the Flotel is the upstairs bar, which boasts ice-cold bottles of Ecuadorian *cerveza* at less than 50¢ each.

◆ 011 5932 2554 130

www.galapagosislands.com/html/flotel_orellana.html

Yacht Hotel

The world's first custom-built yacht hotel is located in the heart of London's historic Royal Victoria Docks, just minutes away from the City Airport and Tower Bridge. Sunborn's Yacht Hotel now offers business and leisure travelers a unique experience, on par with that on the finest cruise ships, without ever leaving port.

◆ 44 (0) 20 7059 9100

www.sunbornhotels.com

Houseboats

A seventy-year-old barge has been converted into a charming houseboat and is moored in the canals of Amsterdam. The two-bedroom, thirty-two-meter boat can accommodate four people.

◆ 31 20 4197255

www.houseboat.nl

Acadia Houseboat Rentals has two houseboats available. Even though these houseboats are permanently moored, they are ideally located near downtown Seattle and can accommodate five to six people for $155 to $195 per day.

◆ (206) 200-8636

www.seattlehouseboatrentals.com

Underwater Hotel

Named in memory of Jules Verne, author of *Twenty Thousand Leagues under the Sea,* this hotel is located off the shore of Key Largo, Florida. Originally built as a research laboratory, Jules' Undersea Lodge is the world's first underwater hotel.

◆ (305) 451-2353

www.jul.com

Volcano Hotel

On the rim of Santorini's dormant volcano rests the charming Perivolas Traditional Houses hotel. There are no TVs, CD players, or DVD players; instead, the hotel promotes itself as a place to come for mental detox. The light, roomy suites are extremely comfortable, with small balconies and patios that overlook the infinity pool and the ocean in the distance.

◆ Perivolas Traditional Houses
Oia, Santorini, Greece
30 22860 71308
www.perivolas.gr

Island Hotel

Hilton's Maldives resort is built on two islands, one of which has
one hundred beach villas, each with its own open-air shower
facing a private garden, encircled by a white, sandy beach. Or
you can go even more upmarket and splurge for one of the forty-
eight water villas on the other island.
◆ 960 450629
www.hilton.com

Cave Hotels

Cave or troglodyte dwellings are found in Southern Europe and
Turkey. People through the ages have been hammering away at
limestone or tufa to make rooms, cathedrals, wine cellars, tombs,
and even hotels. France's Les Haute Roches is a troglodyte hotel
near Tours. Ataman Hotel in Turkey is a two-hundred-year-old
structure carved out of rock in the Cappadocia region. The
House of Wonders, also in Cappadocia, is a restored cave
dwelling.
◆ Cave Hotels in southern Europe and Turkey
www.goeurope.about.com/cs/cavehouses
Les Haute Roches
33 (0) 4 94 71 05 07
www.hotellesroches.com
Ataman Hotel
90 384 271 23 10
www.atamanhotel.com
The House of Wonders
39 051 234 974
www.houseofwonders.com

Built into the side of a hill in Coober Pedy, South Australia, where most of the residents live underground, this hotel offers fifty guest rooms, nineteen of which are subterranean.

◆ 61 8 8672 5688

www.desertcave.com

Earthships

An Earthship is a biotecture home designed to be self-sustaining and reduce the structure's impact on the environment by utilizing recycled materials and solar and photovoltaic power, among other appropriate technologies. Located in Taos, New Mexico, several different rentals are available on a nightly or weekly basis.

◆ (505) 751-0462

www.earthship.org

Tree Houses

An increasingly popular alternative to hotels, tree houses are popping up all over. The Out 'n' About Treesort in Cave Junction, Oregon, is run by a tree house fanatic who boasts he has built the world's largest concentration of arboreal edifices.

◆ (541) 592-2208

www.treehouses.com

Treehouse Cottages, in Eureka Springs, Arkansas, targets the romantic-getaway crowd. River of Life Farm in Dora, Missouri, has tree houses nestled right by the River of Life.

◆ (479) 253-8667

www.treehousecottages.com

(417) 261-7777

www.riveroflifefarm.com

The CedarCreek Treehouse near Seattle is an ecotourism haven with solar power. But beware, there's only one tree house, so book ahead.

◆ (360) 569-2991
www.cedarcreektreehouse.com

Giraffe Manor

Don't be surprised if Lynn or Arlene pokes her spotted head into your second-story bedroom at Giraffe Manor in Nairobi, Kenya. They are two of the Rothschild giraffes that grace the property. Once endangered, these animals have flourished in Langata South, a suburb of Nairobi, and over the years many of the giraffes from Giraffe Manor have moved next door to the Nairobi National Park.
◆ 254 2 891078
www.giraffemanor.com

Mobile Hotel

A customized truck and trailer provide a rare glimpse of the South American countryside and remote villages along the old Estrada Real. Flavio Melo runs Brazil's unique Exploranter, an overland hotel on wheels. The twenty-five-ton Scania truck and trailer that make up the Exploranter's lounge, kitchen, and twenty-eight-berth sleeping quarters can go on the back roads to parts of Brazil that nobody knows.
◆ 55 11 3085 2011
In Portuguese, www.exploranter.com
43 1 892 3877
In English and German, www.eco-tour.org/
travel/trcy_br_226en.html

Jailhouse Inn

The Jailhouse Inn, in Preston, Minnesota, is the old Fillmore County jail, built in the Italianate architecture style in 1869. The inn has a room called the Cell Block, where guests may choose to sleep behind bars just like prisoners. There's also the sheriff's personal bedroom. The Court Room, Bridal Suite, and Cell Block have two-person whirlpools.

◆ (507) 765-2181
www.jailhouseinn.com

Brothel Hotel

In Nevada (where else?), the Wild Horse Canyon Resort offers a unique lodging experience. "I want it to be known as a resort and spa and a fine restaurant that also has a brothel license," says the owner. The parlor is masculine and classic, reminiscent of a library in a men's club or a fine hotel. Leather couches, heavy wooden tables, framed paintings and etchings, and mounted heads of gazelles, elands, and other animals from an African hunt dominate the room where the patrons and the employees meet for the first time. This isn't your average front desk experience—a short distance away is the negotiation room, where prices range widely, depending on the customer's interests.

◆ (775) 343-1224
www.wildhorsenv.com

Nudist Resorts

Central Florida's Pasco County is home to six nudist resorts and has become perhaps the nation's hottest destination for people who would rather be unclothed. An estimated hundred thousand nudists pour into the area each year, and the American Association for Nude Recreation (AANR) boasts a membership of fifty thousand, up 20 percent over the past decade.

◆ www.aanr.com

Popular nudist resorts across the country include upscale places like the Desert Shadows in Palm Springs.

◆ (800) 292-9298 or (760) 325-6410
www.desertshadows.com
The Avalon, West Virginia
(304) 947-5600
www.avalon-nude.com

Paradise Lakes Nudist Resort
(800) 808-8408
www.paradiselakes.com

Monastery Hotels

It's not every day, or even every decade, that a 205-room luxury hotel opens in crowded Venice. So the conversion of a seventh-century monastery on its own seventeen-acre island into the San Clemente Palace is big news in La Serenissima. The twelfth-century ducal chapel is a remembrance of things past, but there have been upgrades that would shock the penitent: Murano glass lamps, terrazzo floors, velvet-and-silk tapestries. Its Mediterranean Ca' dei Frati restaurant features a particularly tempting piece of eye candy: a view of the Campanile beckoning in the distance.
◆ 39 041 244 50 01
In Italian, www.sanclemente.thi.it
In English, www.thi.it/english/hotel/san_clemente/

A peaceful place in Santa Barbara to get away from it all is the affordable retreat at Mount Calvary, a large, Spanish-style house up in the hills outside town, which is actually an old monastery. Mount Calvary welcomes guests of all religions and asks for a donation of $70 per day, which includes bed, bath, linens, and all meals.
◆ (805) 962-9855, ext. 10
www.mount-calvary.org

Convent Hotels

Il Rosario, an Italian convent conveniently located around the corner from the Colosseum in Rome, has forty single and double rooms, some with private baths, for as little as $32 per night per person. Be sure to ask for a wake-up call—a nun will come by in the morning and knock on your door.

◆ Via Sant' Agata dei Gotti 10
00184 Rome, Italy
(39-6) 679-2346
e-mail: irodopre@tin.it

The San Francesco convent, run by a Franciscan order, has six-teen rooms with shared baths for about $30 per person per night. The rooftop terrace overlooks the Vatican walls onto the dome of St. Peter's Basilica.

◆ Via Niccolo V35
Rome, Italy
(39-6) 393-665-31

Hotels for the Overweight

A string of German hotels is being adapted to cater to the extra-large customer. Bedroom doors have been widened, sunbeds rein-forced, and double-size baths fitted. All-day buffets are available, and no attempts are made to entice guests into physical fitness. The Freedom Paradise Club offers guests two four-star hotels and five restaurants at the Riviera Maya in Mexico.

◆ (866) LIVE XXL
www.freedomparadise.com

Zap Nap Pods

Sleep-deprived travelers have a new way to catch up on their z's with the touchdown of Zap Nap Pods at U.S. airports. Similar to Japanese capsule-hotel rooms and based on the cat-carrier design, each rectangular seven- by four- by four-foot pod comes with a comfortable mattress, a pullout TV, a radio, and Internet access. And there's no need to worry about missing your flight—Zap Nap attendants rouse slumberers in time for boarding. Fliers are already snoring at Denver International, with more capsules in the works for other airports, including San Francisco and Atlanta ($10 per half hour).

◆ (866) 803 8769

www.zapnappod.com

Beat Hotel

Want to beat a retreat to the 1950s? Then head to the Beat Hotel—right smack in the California desert. Only eight rooms here, where you can either be creative and interact with the spirits of Jack Kerouac, Allen Ginsberg, and William S. Burroughs or simply create your very own lost weekend. It's actually a restored 1957 motel, complete with photographs taken by Burroughs himself. Even my mother would like this place, since each room comes with a manual typewriter.

◆ (760) 251-6470

www.dhsbeathotel.com

Windmills

England offers a longborrow windmill in the Devonshire countryside, located on four hundred square miles of farmland between the South Horns, Dartmoor, and the sea. The simply furnished windmill can accommodate up to four people.

◆ 44 (0) 1803 316191

www.devonwindmills.co.uk

Villas, Farmhouses, and Castles

The task of deciding on a rental property in Italy has been made a little easier. Choose from charming cottages, extravagant castles and palaces, villas, city apartments, and simple country farmhouses.

◆ (866) 737-0000 or (601) 440-2000

www.papaverorentals.com

Another great resource for villas is the Parker Company, which specializes in more than 350 inviting villas in Italy and elsewhere. Some of these are as large as one hundred rooms (bring lots of friends) and include, thankfully, a staff.

◆ www.theparkercompany.com

Rentvillas.com offers more than three thousand properties in Italy, France, England, Ireland, Scotland, Spain, Portugal, Greece, and Turkey. Properties range from affordable to luxurious, from intimate cottages and rustic farmhouses to thirty-room grand estates.

◆ (800) 726-6702

www.rentvillas.com

Towers

You'll find one on Baron Island, on Murcia, part of the Costa Calida of Spain. Designed by Frank Lloyd Wright, this hilltop watchtower folly is located thirty minutes from the mainland.

◆ Vladi Private Islands Gmblt

(49) (40) 33 89 89

www.vladi-private-islands.de

Fall Mountain Lookout, in Malheur National Forest in John Day in eastern Oregon, was built in 1930 by the Civilian Conservation Corps (CCC). This fourteen- by fourteen-foot cabin sits atop a twenty-five-foot tower at an elevation of 5,949 feet. Known in the Forest Register as a historic lookout, it was abandoned in the mid-1980s. This old fire watchtower comes with an electric cookstove, refrigerator, heater, and lights, and a futon bed. It can sleep two comfortably, but keep in mind that there is no water and no indoor rest room (a vault toilet is located in close proximity to the lookout). The cabin is available in spring and summer (dates vary depending on snowfall). The price is $25 per night, which goes toward maintaining the tower.

◆ (541) 575-3000

www.fs.fed.us/r6/malheur, click on "Recreational Rentals"

Dormitories

During the summer and winter months, college dorms can be an inexpensive alternative to hotels. The London School of Economics has several dorms to choose from. Singles are £27 and doubles go for £38 per night.

◆ 44 (0) 20 7955 7575

www.lse.ac.uk/collections/vacations.dates.htm

Hosteling in the Big City

You might think that a visit to New York City would break any budget, but Hosteling International New York offers lodging for only $24 per night. The hostel, a historic building on Manhattan's Upper West Side, has even more to offer than its inexpensive overnight rate. Discounts have been arranged for restaurants, comedy clubs, music clubs, off Broadway theater, and more.

◆ (301) 495-1240

www.hiayh.org

Library Hotel

This Manhattan hotel is dedicated to the different categories of knowledge classified by the Dewey Decimal System. Each of the sixty rooms is filled with books and artwork related to a particular topic, such as zoology on the math and science floor and geography and travel on the history floor. More than sixty thousand books, ranging from erotica to Edgar Allan Poe constitute the Library Hotel's eclectic collection.

◆ 299 Madison Avenue at 41st Street
New York, NY 10017
(212) 983-4500, toll-free (877) 793-7323
www.libraryhotel.com

Theme Hotels

The well-known Chelsea Star Hotel is a fun-filled fantasy ideal for the young (or young at heart), where the choice of creative and unique rooms showcases a variety of eras, themes, and stars, including rooms dedicated to *Star Trek*, Madame Butterfly, Cleopatra, and Madonna (where the pop star actually lived when she was a struggling artist—the room now contains much of her memorabilia). In addition, the shared bathrooms are bright, and the hallways are colorful and sun-splashed. The hotel is situated in the heart of Manhattan, so it is easily accessible to all major city attractions. Room prices are extremely reasonable.

◆ (212) 244-7827

www.starhotelny.com

The Pavilion Fashion Rock 'n' Roll Hotel is a groovy thirty-room hotel in central London, targeted at a discerning, artistically minded clientele. Rooms are themed to project a funky and glamorous image. Honky Tonky Afro is a tribute to the 1970s, while Casablanca Nights is a deco-inspired, Moorish fantasy, and "Enter the Dragon" is a mystical cocktail of oriental treasures. Rooms are crammed with quirky eccentricities and benefit from having all the necessities of modern-day living such as en suite facilities, direct-dial telephones, and satellite television.

◆ 44 20 8800 1102 (outside U.K.)

www.londonlodging.co.uk/hotels/west/Pavilion

Rooms at the Viva Las Vegas Villas Hotel include the glamorous Elvis and Priscilla pink Cadillac bedroom in gold and hot pink accented by the King's memorabilia. There is a room based on Camelot, featuring a drawbridge bed with lots of medieval touches; a Marilyn Monroe room; and a Blue Hawaii room, complete with a tiki hut bath, island scenery, and palm tree bedposts to make you feel like you're sleeping on the beach. The coolest room may be the Austin Powers suite, decorated with beaded doorways, lava lamps, and a groovy shag carpet.

◆ (800) 574-4450 or (702) 384-0771

www.vivalasvegasvillas.com

Home Exchanges

For those who want to totally immerse themselves in another culture without paying steep hotel prices—and for those who are willing to take a chance on people who are also willing to take a chance on them—there's the concept of the home exchange. For example, you might exchange your home in Arizona with that of a family in a small town in Austria. You stay in their house; they stay in yours. Cost: hardly anything, since you are exchanging homes.

For the prices stated, you can list your own home with the following directories:

◆ Intervac US, San Francisco, CA
10,000 listings, 80 percent international
(800) 756-4663
www.intervacus.com
$78 per year
Home Link International, Key West, FL
15,000 listings, 60 percent in Europe, 25 percent in North America, the rest in Hawaii, Australia, New Zealand, and the Caribbean
(800) 638-3841
www.homelink.org
$78 per year
Trading Homes International, Hermosa Beach, CA
2,000 properties, 50 percent international
(310) 798-3864
www.homexchange.com
$50 per year
The Invented City, San Francisco, CA
2,000 properties, 50 percent international
(800) 788-2489
www.invented-city.com
$50 per year
International Home Exchange Network
(386) 238-3633

www.ihen.com
$29.95 per year membership
Holiday Home Exchanges in the United Kingdom
44 (0) 1756 749966
www.dialanexchange.com
Seniors Home Exchange
www.seniorshomeexchange.com
$65 per three-year membership, $45 for AARP members
Apartment Home Exchanges
(800)-528-2010 or (303) 759-9901
www.apartmentfinders.com

GAY/LESBIAN TRAVEL TRIPS

You've done Provincetown, Michigan, Key West, Sydney, San Francisco, and the Dinah Shore. You've eaten beignets in New Orleans and sunned on Sappho Island. Stumped for ideas for your next adventure? Here are twenty excellent travel websites, ranging from mainstream to extreme adventure, for gays/lesbians:

www.womenfest.com
www.planetout.com/travel/calendar
www.adventureassociates.net
www.adventureboundmen.com
www.goodadventure.com
www.alysonadventure.com
www.coda-tours.com
www.davidtours.com
www.footprintstravel.com
www.womansplace.com
www.kalani.com
www.mariahwe.com
www.outwestadventures.com
www.spiritjourneys.com
www.tototours.com

www.underseax.com
www.ventureout.com
www.womantours.com
www.worldsapart.com
www.outandabout.com

TRAVEL AND HOTELS FOR PEOPLE WITH DISABILITIES

> Someone who is visually impaired would never want to stay
> at a hotel with a complex floorplan. You go down a hall, up
> an elevator, down a hall—it's like a maze. For someone vi-
> sually impaired or blind, who's trying to get from the lobby
> to the room and to the restaurant, a more traditional layout
> would be easier, rather than trying to get all fancy.
>
> —Maria Runyan
> Five-time Paralympic gold medalist and
> the first blind American athlete to compete in the Olympics

It has always amazed me how many hotels are not in full compliance with the Americans with Disabilities Act (ADA), more
than a decade after it became the law of the land. And in a society where money talks, believe me when I tell you that people
who are physically challenged are not silent.

Consider this: a study by the Open Doors Organization, the
Travel Industry Association of America (TIA), and the Society
for Accessible Travel and Hospitality (SATH) suggests that annual travel spending by people with disabilities would nearly
double, to approximately $27 billion per year, if certain needs
were met.

Among the needs that would have to be addressed are lodging issues, including the availability of guest rooms that are close
to property amenities and staff members who will go out of their
way to accommodate guests with disabilities. Open Doors, TIA,

and SATH further suggest that people with disabilities could generate $8.4 billion for the lodging industry alone if their travel needs were better addressed.

More than fifty million Americans have some kind of disability, making them the largest minority group in the country. Until recently, and especially before passage of the ADA, they were not well treated by the travel industry, and numerous vacation possibilities were effectively barred to them.

In addition to being snubbed by the travel industry, a recent survey found that 28 percent of people with a severe disability live below the poverty level, making travel even more difficult.

Because of a growing national sensitivity to the plight of people with disabilities, reflected not merely in words but in legislation, the situation is today improving, though much remains to be done. The following companies offer thousands of people with disabilities the chance to enjoy the rewards of travel.

Search Beyond Adventures, Inc.

Aside from its large repertoire of destinations and tours, this company's forte is its ability to match disabled travelers with just the right-sized group—the appropriate staff-to-vacationer ratio—to suit their needs and level of independence. Group sizes range from four to thirty travelers, but the staff-to-vacationer ratios range from only one-to-two to one-to-four.
◆ www.searchbeyond.com

Catholic Travel Office

CTO arranges for persons with disabilities to travel to Lourdes and other Catholic shrines in Europe. Each fall it operates a large group trip (usually about three hundred people) to Lourdes for persons with disabilities. Accompanying the group are doctors, nurses, and paramedics.
◆ www.catholictravels.com

Wilderness Inquiry

The primary focus of Wilderness Inquiry is to integrate tourists with disabilities with the able-bodied, for vacations in which everyone learns about nature and each other. Wilderness Inquiry hosts people of all levels and types of disabilities, including quadriplegics, deaf persons, blind persons, and the developmentally disabled.

◆ www.wildernessinquiry.com

Jubilee Sailing Trust

A mix of able-bodied and disabled passengers regularly embark on sailing adventures aboard the *Tenacious* and the *Lord Nelson*, two huge nineteenth-century-style vessels. Most participants with disabilities use wheelchairs, but a variety of people with disabilities take part.

◆ www.jst.org.uk

Access Adventures

Access Adventures plans five hundred to six hundred vacations for a broad variety of handicapped travelers per year, including a recent trip for a paraplegic customer who wanted to visit his childhood home in India and a woman with a circulatory disorder—she could not sit or stand for more than two hours at a time—who wanted to take her family to Australia.

◆ (716) 889-9096.

Yates Travel

An expert in cruises, Rochelle Yates recently arranged a cruise to Bermuda for two 94-year-old passengers, which she considers her greatest triumph. Yates specializes in the cruise needs of a wide variety of persons with disabilities and in the similar needs of elderly persons.

◆ (800) 545-8327

www.yatestravel.com

Wheel Coach Services, Inc.

Travelers with disabilities including dialysis needs, those with restricted movement, or those who are simply slow walkers can enjoy a tour of the beautiful island of St. Croix by way of Wheel Coach Services. Wheel Coach specializes in tours of the island custom-designed by the client. Usually the tour involves a scenic drive and visits to a rum factory, a sugar plantation, and a botanical garden.

◆ www.wheelcoach.com

Society for Accessible Travel and Hospitality

For travelers with disabilities that are not described in the foregoing discussion, contact SATH, whose experts can usually suggest a source of assistance.

◆ www.sath.org

PETS AND HOTELS

Twenty-nine million people, or 14 percent of Americans, have traveled with their pets more than fifty miles, according to a 2001 survey by the Travel Industry Association of America. Most people with companion animals regard them as their children; hence, they love hotels and resorts that openly welcome them. However, along with the welcome comes responsibility on the part of the pet owner.

Ten Commandments for Pets and Guests

1. Always call ahead.
2. Always declare your pet at check-in.
3. There's a place for everything.
4. "Do not disturb" means exactly that—and this applies from the inside of a guest room as well as from outside.
5. Bring extra towels.

6. Don't leave the pet alone.
7. Bring bedding.
8. If your animal sheds, bring a battery-powered vacuum cleaner.
9. Schedule feeding time such that you can also schedule walking time when it won't bother other guests.
10. *Management's word is gospel!*

Oh yes, there's also an eleventh commandment: a pet-friendly hotel is a great idea if you have a pet (or are a pet). But if you're the guest arriving *after* a guest with a pet has left, the hotel has a responsibility to disclose that a pet has previously occupied your room. This is important for a number of reasons: you may have allergies; pets can often carry diseases and ticks; and, perhaps most disturbing, during random blacklight tests of hotel rooms, large urine stains were found on many room carpets, and these stains were discovered nowhere near bathrooms. The evidence suggests animals as the culprits.

Having said this, there are hotels that do an excellent, responsible job of welcoming pets and their owners, as well as guests who travel without animals. Here are my favorites.

Loews (Multiple Locations)

The Loews Loves Pets program was started in 2000 and has grown to include nineteen hotels in the Loews chain. At check-in, guests receive a welcome note from the general manager listing available pet services, as well as recommended dog-walking routes, pet shops, and pet-friendly restaurants. Specialized bedding for dogs and cats is set up in advance, along with a bag of treats, a toy, place mats with food and water bowls, and a "do not disturb" sign to alert housekeeping that a pet is in the room. A special room service menu includes bottled water and milk, grilled lamb for dogs, grilled liver for cats, and vegetarian choices for both.

◆ (800) 23-LOEWS

www.loewshotels.com

Hotel ZaZa (Dallas, Texas)

Features at this posh Dallas hotel include pet toys and treats, a special pet lounge, a pet vacation DVD, a pet diary, and an exclusive oil portrait of your beloved pet. Other fabulous features of this $5,000 package include in-room breakfast and dinner for two with that special companion, a canine-walking service twice daily, an in-room kennel, and, naturally, designer VIP food and water bowls for guests to keep.

◆ (214) 468-8399

www.hotelzaza.com

Relais and Chateaux (Multiple Locations)

Properties include the Little Nell in Aspen, Colorado, where dogs get special treats at turndown time, and the Old Drovers Inn in Dover Plains, New York, where dogs are treated to cookies upon arrival and a walk through the local park, and where the culinary team is prepared to serve a pet's favorite dish upon the request of the owners. Other Relais and Chateaux hotels are the Point, in Saranac Lake, New York, where dogs and cats can walk in the Adirondack Mountains; the San Ysidro Ranch, Montecito, Santa Barbara, California, which has a special doggie dinner menu that includes steak and chopped beef.

◆ (212) 856-0115

www.integra.fr/relaisechateaux.com

Hotel Lancaster (Paris, France)

For €90 a night, this five-star hotel will place a luxurious doggie bed in your room. The Lancaster also offers these beds (engraved with the dog's name) for sale from €960 to €1,040.

◆ www.hotel-lancaster.fr

Hotel Telluride (Telluride, Colorado)

Amenities include a welcome bag and pet treats at check-in, plenty of room to walk on or near the property, and pickup receptacles located throughout the town.

◆ (970) 369-1188

www.thehoteltelluride.com

Paw House (West Rutland, Vermont)

A bed-and-breakfast in Vermont that caters to dog lovers and their pets, this historic eighteenth-century farmhouse offers first-class accommodations, fantastic amenities, and the peace of mind that responsible dog owners deserve. There is a 1,200-square-foot Mario's playhouse for dogs, a doggie menu that includes doggie biscuits, special beds, and even room service.

◆ www.pawhouseinn.com

Ritz-Carlton (Coconut Grove, Florida)

Now offering a "Bow-Wow Butler" service, this hotel greets and escorts the guests' dogs to a room with a dog bed, toys, and a water bowl. Also, a welcome note from the general manager is placed in the room. Later, the Bow-Wow Butler will walk the dog on-site for exercise, then take the dog in style via town car to a local groomer. Finally, the butler and dog will return to the room for a special doggie cuisine called "poochie sushi." All this isn't cheap (roughly $500), but if you are a guest and do not hire the butler service, the hotel will still deliver a special bed and water bowl to the pooch.

◆ www.ritzcarlton.com

Hotel Monaco (Denver, Colorado)

At check-in, guests can request a goldfish delivered to their room that the staff will take care of feeding. The hotel director of pet relations—a three-year-old Jack Russell terrier named Lilly—greets guests in the lobby, and each pet receives a dog

treat upon check-in. There are no height or weight limits for pets, and walks, supervised by hotel staff, are available. The new "Dog Daze" package includes hotel accommodations, a dog-walking map, food and water dishes, a bag of treats, a dog poo bag, and a $5 donation to an animal care foundation.
◆ www.monaco-denver.com

Hôtel de Crillon (Paris, France)

This is one of the grand hotels of the world. It has hosted dozens of celebrities and world leaders, including Emperor Hirohito of Japan, King George V of England, Sir Winston Churchill, and presidents Herbert Hoover, Theodore Roosevelt, and Richard Nixon since it opened in the first decade of the twentieth century. It also treats its dogs like royalty.

Check out the Dog de Crillon. Pets receive complimentary accommodations with an array of services including souvenir collars with the Crillon logo, name tags, and room service, as well as special custom-sized sleeping baskets in the master's room. And for those walks around the famous Place de la Concorde, the concierge staff will take Fido, leash in hand. Your dog even gets a specialized canine menu from room service, including "thinly sliced breast of poultry with assorted vegetables."

Guest rooms and suites have been restored in Louis XV style under the auspices of the French National Historic Landmark Commission.
◆ 10, Place de la Concorde
F-75008 Paris
www.hoteldecrillon.com

Fairmont Royal York (Toronto, Canada)

The Fairmont offers the "Very Important Pet" package, which includes a stay in a specially designed, pet-friendly room and a welcome kit that consists of dog treats, food bowls, extra towels, and a custom blanket. Owners can order room service for their hungry pets, and the hotel provides information on the best spots in the area to walk your dog.

◆ (800) 441-1414

www.fairmont.com

Inn by the Sea (Portland, Oregon)

This little inn offers condo-style suites with ocean views. What's great about this place is that you and your pet can enjoy it, as the little inn offers pet-friendly accommodations and even a room service menu for your furry friend.

◆ www.innbythesea.com

Index

ABOUT THE AUTHOR

PETER GREENBERG is the travel editor for NBC's *Today* show. He is also the chief correspondent for the Discovery Network's Travel Channel, editor-at-large of *National Geographic Traveler* magazine, as well as a regular contributor to CNBC and MSNBC. He can be seen often on *The Oprah Winfrey Show*. He lives in Los Angeles, New York, and Bangkok, when he's not living in hotels.